M000199081

LONDON'S

SECRET SQUARE MILE

LONDON'S

SECRET SQUARE MILE

DAVID LONG

FOREWORD BY THE RT HON. THE LORD MAYOR OF
LONDON, ALDERMAN WILLIAM RUSSELL

The
History
Press

First published 2011 as *Hidden City*
This edition first published 2021

The History Press
97 St George's Place, Cheltenham,
Gloucestershire, GL50 3QB
www.thehistorypress.co.uk

© David Long, 2011, 2021
All illustrations © Melissa Turland, 2021

The right of David Long to be identified as the Author
of this work has been asserted in accordance with the
Copyright, Designs and Patents Act 1988.

All rights reserved. No part of this book may be reprinted
or reproduced or utilised in any form or by any electronic,
mechanical or other means, now known or hereafter invented,
including photocopying and recording, or in any information
storage or retrieval system, without the permission in writing
from the Publishers.

British Library Cataloguing in Publication Data.
A catalogue record for this book is available from the British Library.

ISBN 978 0 7509 9717 1

Typesetting and origination by The History Press
Printed and bound in Great Britain by TJ Books Limited, Padstow, Cornwall.

Trees for Lᵾfe

CONTENTS

FOREWORD

In order to survive, cities must change and adapt to accommodate the evolving needs of their inhabitants. The City of London is no different, constituting an exceptional blend of the new and the old, and telling the story of its rich history through its winding alleys and bustling roads. With new architecture rising high above the City's streets, David Long's fantastic book tells the story of the hidden squares, the concealed courtyards and the meandering passages that make this great City so unique.

It is in a city's survival that many of the greatest tales lie – stories of struggle and resilience that have ensured roads continue to run and buildings stand tall. Following both the Great Fire of London and the destruction wreaked by the Blitz, there were proposals to overhaul the City's blueprint and start over. However, these calls were resisted, and we are so grateful for those that spoke out – we have those brave voices to thank today as we tread the very same footsteps of the thousands that came before us.

As the 692nd Lord Mayor of the City of London, I believe strongly in the importance of our City's history and uncovering the many tales that lie within. After all, it is only in understanding the significance of our past that we can strive towards a stronger future. As we continue to tackle the challenges presented by the Covid-19 pandemic, I am overwhelmingly proud of our unique City and all those within it that have responded with courage and resilience. Indeed, the tales of the past year will form another footnote in the story of the City of London, but the fundamental strengths of our City will be vital as we recover and rebuild, and our ancient foundations will again play a crucial role – reminding us of the many challenges that we have overcome.

The Rt Hon. The Lord Mayor of London
Alderman William Russell
January 2021

INTRODUCTION

'I came suddenly upon such knotty problems of alleys, such enigmatical entries, and such sphinx's riddles of streets without thoroughfares, as must, I conceive, baffle the audacity of porters, and confound the intellects of hackney-coachmen. I could almost have believed, at times, that I must be the first discoverer of some of these *terrae incognitae*, and doubted whether they had yet been laid down in the modern charts of London.'

Thomas De Quincey,
Confessions of an English Opium-Eater (1821)

Insulated from the noise, from the seemingly endless development and redevelopment of the historic Square Mile – and above all from the aggressively commercial bustle of the larger streets and traffic-clogged thoroughfares – is a second, almost secret City of London.

Comprising a sometimes bewildering tangle of narrow alleyways, courtyards and unexpected dead-ends, many of them medieval in origin even if they sadly no longer give this impression, this second, secret city is a compact but intriguing place. Dotted with blue plaques and strange statues and memorials to the forgotten, often leading the explorer to little gardens built around Roman remains and derelict or discarded churches, this maze of little cut-throughs, shortcuts and byways conceals many old and even timber-framed buildings which have somehow survived against the odds, and offers walkers the chance to stumble upon some of the most unexpected and charming places to eat and drink in central London.

Above all, though, to appropriate the words of John Clare, one of London's many biographers, it is somewhere 'you discover that commonplace traffic, the swinish rush of metal, is happening somewhere else'. Also, to quote Peter Ackroyd, somewhere one begins to understand how the area stretching from Tower to Temple really is 'made for walking ... a city of small streets and sudden vistas, of unexpected alleys and hidden courtyards which cannot be seen from a bus or car'.

Though famously rebuilt after the Great Fire of 1666, and again and again in the centuries which followed, the basic streetscape of London's financial heart still reflects its medieval layout – and it is this that best conveys the oft-cited impression of it being truly a city within a city. The old gateways into the bustling medieval settlement may be long gone, the Roman wall has almost entirely (but not quite) disappeared beneath warehouses, offices and apartments, and towering new developments continue to be thrown up and torn down with bewildering rapidity. But stepping behind the modern façades, or squeezing through narrow passages between the vast glass ziggurats of twenty-first-century commerce in search of a favourite Wren church or simply somewhere quieter to sit and think, it is still possible to come upon something ancient or timeless, and to enjoy the precious thrill of discovering somewhere centuries old yet to the beholder all but unknown.

'I have seen the West End, the parks, the fine squares; but I love the City far better. The City seems so much more in earnest; its business, its rush, its roar, are such serious things, sights, sounds. The City is getting its living – the West End but enjoying its pleasure. At the West End you may be amused; but in the City you are deeply excited.'

Charlotte Brontë, *Villette* (1853)

SECRET CITY

CITY

STREET BY STREET

ABCHURCH YARD, EC4

Documented as long ago as the twelfth century, at which time it was known variously as Abchurch, Abbechurch, Habechirch and Apechurch. Each is almost certainly a corruption of 'upchurch', a reference to the rising ground on which the neighbouring church of St Mary Abchurch was built, or to the fact that the church was upriver from the much larger St Mary Overie (now Southwark Cathedral). This last named had been its mother foundation until the patronage was transferred to Corpus Christi College, Cambridge, during the reign of Elizabeth I.

What we see now, a small geometrically cobbled yard with circular stonework, was originally the graveyard – to one side of which wartime bombing revealed a fourteenth-century crypt – but in the way of such places it now provides a relatively peaceful spot on Abchurch Lane where office workers can kick off their shoes at lunchtime.

The church itself, with its elegant, shallow, painted dome, is regarded as one of Wren's prettiest, and also among the most original, even though the fabric sustained severe damage during the aforementioned bombing. The Grinling Gibbons reredos, for example, is particularly magnificent and is the only one in the City with documented proof of its complete authenticity. That said, it took five years to restore after being blown into more than 2,000 pieces during one particular raid. If the church is open, take a look at the churchwardens' pews too, which were designed to incorporate sword rests and dog kennels beneath the seats – both once common enough features but which nowadays are only very rarely seen.

ADAMS COURT, EC2

Reached through an uninspiring looking archway on Old Broad Street or via a somewhat pompous little courtyard opening off Threadneedle Street, this court takes its name from one Thomas Adams (1586–1668) who lived here in the 1640s when he was Master of the Drapers' Company. With the company's hall located in nearby Throgmorton Avenue since the purchase of the site from Henry VII a century earlier, Alderman Adams went on to become Lord Mayor in 1645.

The court meanders into Fountain Court and, with its immaculate little greensward overlooked by the City of London Club, the place provides a perfect refuge from the hubbub of the City. As such it provides a most marked contrast to how it would have been in Thomas Adams' day when (as a consequence of his support for the Royalist cause during the Civil War) it was to be the scene of his arrest.

His house on the site was ransacked by Roundheads searching for the king, and he himself was locked in the Tower. Unlike so many others, he survived this ordeal, and later helped to restore the monarchy. At the war's conclusion he was rewarded with a baronetcy.

ADDLE HILL, EC4

Now just a short cul-de-sac off Carter Lane, the hill is thought to mark the location of the home of a Saxon nobleman, its name coming from the Saxon *adel*, meaning noble or a prince. In medieval times it was more colourfully known as Adhelingestrate or Athelingestrate but, just as Stow noted little of interest in 1598 – 'In Addle Street or Lane I find no monuments' – there is little here today to detain the traveller.

Curiously, the similarly named Addle Street, EC2, has a less noble connection, being derived from the Old English word for filth or dung.

ALDERMAN'S WALK, EC2

Shown on many older maps as Dashwood Walk, in the seventeenth century this was a passageway leading to the large house and gardens of Sir Francis Dashwood. A Member of the Common Council of the City, his son succeeded to the title of Baron le Despencer and later served as Chancellor of the Exchequer by which time the name had been changed.

On its southern side the Walk adjoins the churchyard of St Botolph-without-Bishopsgate, where in 1413 a female hermit subsisted on a pension of 40s a year. Bordering the churchyard at that time was a ditch, described a hundred years or so later – by which time the smell was being blamed on Frenchmen living nearby – as being full of 'soilage of houses, with other filthiness cast into the ditch … to the danger of impoisoning the whole city'.

St Botolph's itself is one of four City churches dedicated to this seventh-century patron saint of travellers, and for this reason was positioned hard by the City gates. Three of the four survived the Great Fire, but being generally decrepit this particular one was eventually pulled down and then replaced in 1725 at a cost of £10,400 by a new one designed by George Dance the Elder and his father-in-law James Gould.

One weekend in 1982 a ghost, apparently, in the church carelessly wandered in front of a camera and allowed its owner,

Chris Brackley, to take a picture. Unaware of this at the time, Brackley found an image of a woman in old-fashioned clothing standing on the balcony when he developed the picture.

St Botolph's also once oversaw a charity school for fifty poor boys and girls, and although its two decorative Coade stone figures of charity children have now been removed from the front of the building, the old schoolroom can still be seen in the attractive churchyard to the west of the church.

The poet John Keats was christened here in 1795, as was the actor, benefactor and 'Master Overseer and Ruler of the Bears, Bulls and Mastiff Dogs' Edward Alleyn. Sir Paul Pindar, the façade of whose mansion is preserved at the Victoria and Albert Museum, was a parishioner. The memorial cross in the churchyard is believed to be the first Great War memorial in the country, having been erected in 1916 following the Battle of Jutland and the death of Lord Kitchener.

AMEN CORNER, EC4

No known connection with the 1960s band of the same name, but more likely derived, as suggested by John Carey in an 1828 edition of the *Gentleman's Magazine*, from the words recited by the clergy of the medieval St Paul's as they marched in a procession through the City:

> Let us suppose processioners mustered and marshalled at upper end of Paternoster Row next Cheapside. These commence to march westward, and begin to chant the 'Paternoster', continued this the whole length of the street (thence Paternoster Row). On arrival at [the] bottom of the

street they enter Ave Maria Lane, at the same time beginning to chant the 'Salutation of the Virgin' or 'Ave Maria' which continues until reaching Ludgate Hill, and crossing over to Creed Lane. They there commence the chant of the 'Credo', which continues until they reach the spot now called Amen Corner, where they sing the concluding Amen.

Several doorways in the court still have old-fashioned link extinguishers from the days when residents would pay so-called link boys to run ahead of them lighting the path with a torch or link. These would be extinguished upon arrival, whereupon the boy would take off in search of another 'fare'.

AMEN COURT, EC4

Sharing its origins with the aforementioned Amen Corner, Amen Court for many years provided accommodation for the scribes, residentiary canons and minor canons gathered around St Paul's Cathedral.

Unfortunately, a quite solid-looking, three-storey redbrick gatehouse on Warwick Lane guards the way into this small, secluded enclave with its central but secret garden; admission is only possible by prior application to the Dean and Chapter of St Paul's Cathedral. Alternatively, one might sneak a peep, in which case take a look at the Minor Canons' House and Nos 1–3 which was once home to the great wit Sydney Smith – Hesketh Pearson's *Smith of Smiths* – who was a canon of St Paul's in the 1830s, and later to R.H. Barham who penned the *Ingoldsby Legends*.

The large wall visible through the main archway, incidentally, conceals a grisly remnant of the old Newgate Gaol, the rest having been swept away during the construction of the Central Criminal Court (or Old Bailey, reached via a pretty garden and the semi-subterranean Warwick Passage). Concealed behind the wall is the narrow passage known as Deadman's Walk, along which the condemned were taken to their executions. Afterwards many were buried beneath it and today ghost-hunters refer to it as one of the most haunted spots within the Square Mile. Especially popular is the 'Black Dog of Newgate', which sounds like a pub but is the name given to a shadowy apparition recorded hereabouts. Apparently on more than one occasion – to the accompanying sensory delights of a hideous smell and the sound of human feet dragging along the cobbles – a large black shape has been observed seething and slithering and slobbering along the top of the wall. For those with a taste for such things its origins are said to lie with a case of cannibalism in the gaol during a famine in the time of Henry II, the victim having adopted canine form before returning to haunt those who had feasted off him.

AMERICA SQUARE, EC3

Actually more of a crescent and sadly now largely obliterated by Fenchurch Street station and its Victorian façade. It was laid out in the 1670s as part of a scheme by George Dance the Elder and named in honour of Britain's colonial possession, perhaps in the hope of attracting ships' officers and middle-class merchants with transatlantic connections to move here.

Today its most striking feature is at No. 1, reputedly the first London skyscraper to exploit the 'air rights' over open rail tracks by building over the platforms with a new station entrance incorporated into the development. Granite-clad and with a large roof garden and terraces fifteen storeys above street level, the building itself was completed in 1991 in a deliberately 1920s art deco style with an entrance reminiscent of the Chrysler Building in New York.

ANCHOR YARD, EC1

Far larger in the eighteenth century than now, when it would have had an opening wide enough to admit dray carts delivering ale to the popular Anchor Tavern nearby. Today, on this unlovely stretch of Old Street, there is little of interest besides pretty little Wenlake Cottage which fortunately falls within the St Luke's Conservation Area.

ANGEL COURT, EC2

A modest cut-through from Copthall Avenue to Throgmorton Street, the name comes from the long-gone Angel Tavern although the yard is now better remembered for Birch's Wine House. Tradition has it that, for more than a century, the soup course was prepared here for the annual Lord Mayor's Banquet at Mansion House, although one wonders why such an establishment was unable to knock up a few gallons of its own …

From the mid 1970s the court was dominated by a twenty-one-storey octagonal tower, expensively shod in purple Dakota marble and formerly the London home of J.P. Morgan. Built on land owned by the Worshipful Company of Clothworkers (see Dunster Court, p. 80), it surrounded an internal courtyard containing two old plaques marked *St X B 1796* and *1867 SCS*. These are parish markers denoting the boundary between St Stephen Coleman Street and St Bartholomew-by-the-Exchange.

ANGEL PASSAGE, EC4

One of only two survivors of the several dozen Angel Alleys, Angel Courts, Angel Passages and Angel Yards which once bore testament to the popularity of this particular name for so many City taverns. Angel Passage is also now a very rare survivor of another sort, of the myriad tiny thoroughfares which as recently as Edwardian times thronged the area between the river and busy Upper Thames Street.

Today, even so, it has little to recommend it: nothing indeed besides (at its southern end) Waterman's Walk and Oystergate Walk which provide a number of excellent vantage points to see the Thames and its bridges and the dominating tower of Southwark Cathedral.

ANGEL PLACE, SE1

In the rambling preface to his *Little Dorrit*, Dickens describes:

A certain adjacent Angel Court, leading to Bermondsey, [where] I came to Marshalsea Place, the houses in which I recognised, not only as the great block of the former prison … Whosoever goes into Marshalsea Place, turning out of Angel Court, leading to Bermondsey, will find his feet on the very paving-stones of the extinct Marshalsea Gaol; will see its narrow yard to the right and to the left, very little altered if at all, except that the walls were lowered when the place got free; will look upon the rooms in which the debtors lived; will stand among the crowded ghosts of many miserable years.

Later renamed Angel Place, which is a shame as the Marshalsea name is now highly evocative, the Court was once owned by one Richard Fulmerston. He ran the Angel Tavern which contained a room set aside for use as a private prison cell – an unusual facility eventually superseded by a purpose-built gaol – whose inmates were to include the writers Tobias Smollet and John Wilkes. Fulmerston sold it to the Crown for use by the Marshal of the King's Bench. A former Lord Mayor, John Wilkes is commemorated by a bronze statue on the corner of Fetter Lane and New Fetter Lane, the only cross-eyed statue in the capital, perhaps because, when not being imprisoned, the subject was active as a politician, a polemicist and sometime pornographer.

ARTILLERY LANE, E1

For a long time, the lane led to the sixteenth-century Tasel Close Artillery Yard (see Artillery Passage, p. 23), an area used by gunnery officers of the Tower of London and members of the Honourable Artillery Company from the Dissolution until its sale in 1682.

On the corner of Gun Street a block has been built behind the windowless skeleton of an older, surviving façade, and in the 1700s Dr Johnson was recommending a walk from Charing Cross to Whitechapel, promising his friend he would see along the way 'the greatest series of shops in the world'. While he did

not identify these any further, it is possible that he was referring to this place, in particular No. 56, with its Doric columns and twin curved windows an exemplar of Georgian retailing, and No. 58 which, while refronted since Johnson's day, is still exceedingly handsome.

By the beginning of the twentieth century the area was again *terra incognita*, however. When the writer Jack London visited England in 1902, he put up at Highgate and contacted the offices of Thomas Cook for information about how to arrange a visit to the East End. Back came the reply that the travel agent was unable to help, its representative admitting he knew nothing of this unexplored quarter of the capital. Left to his own devices the author decided to don a disguise as a sailor and just dive in. Sleeping rough on the streets, the experience was to provide valuable research for his book *People of the Abyss*.

ARTILLERY PASSAGE, E1

Following the dissolution by Henry VIII of the hospital and priory of St Mary Spital – founded in 1197 in the area we know today as Spitalfields – a portion of the land on which it stood was set aside as somewhere for Fat Hal's militia or 'Trained Bands' to hone and perfect their gunnery skills.

Charged with defending the City during the Tudor period, the Tower Ordnance and the Guild of St George (also known as the Gentlemen of the Artillery Garden, forerunners of today's Honourable Artillery Company) quickly set to work. Stow, visiting the site while composing his *Survey*, observed that the ground which had formerly been popular with clothworkers keen 'to shoot for games at the popingay' now 'being inclosed with a brick wall, serveth to be an artillery yard, whereunto the gunners of the Tower do weekly repair, namely, every Thursday; and there levelling certain brass pieces of the great artillery against a butt of earth, made for that purpose, they discharge them for their exercise.'

Despite all this Artillery Passage was still known locally as Tasel Close, the name coming from the prickly teazles which were favoured by Spitalfields' population of French Huguenot weavers, who used them to comb and prepare their cloth.

Eventually the more martial name was adopted, however, and in time the Honourable Artillery Company moved to the premises they still occupy on City Road. In 1680 the Tower Ordnance too moved on, their practice sessions now considered potentially too injurious to the growing local population. Within two years the artillery yard had been built over, and nothing remains of it now but the names of several local thoroughfares – Gun Street, Artillery Lane and Fort Street – and a bar called Grapeshots.

ASHENTREE COURT, EC4

The Carmelite order of White Friars – so-named because of the white mantle worn over their brown habits – arrived in London from the Holy Land after being driven from Mount Carmel by the Saracens. Swapping the life of hermits for that of mendicants (and so required to live and work among the people) they occupied a large site stretching from Fleet Street down to the river.

Settled here from about 1240 until the Dissolution in 1538, they were traditionally popular with the people of London and as a consequence were largely left alone during the Peasants' Revolt. For a short while the order even retained a right of sanctuary after the Dissolution, but eventually they were to share the fate of the Black and Grey Friars. Once the instruction went out to 'pull down to the grounds all the walls of the churches, stepulls, cloysters, fraterys, dorters, chapterhowsys', nothing above ground remained of the White Friars although, amazingly, their beautiful crypt was somehow to survive beneath the old *News of the World* building in Bouverie Street (see also Magpie Alley, p. 126, and Britton's Court, p. 45).

Their name is still commemorated in nearby Carmelite Street and Whitefriars Street, but otherwise we are left only with little Ashentree Court. While it lacks trees today, it stands on the site of one of the priory cloisters so at one time would have been laid out in a quadrangle, somewhere for the friars to walk and think.

AUSTIN FRIARS, EC2

An obvious religious connection, the name is a peculiarly English contraction of the Augustinian foundation which was established in the mid-thirteenth century by the 2nd Earl of Hereford, Humphrey de Bohun, whose 'begging friars' rapidly accumulated considerable wealth and property. The Dissolution saw their London properties confiscated by the Crown and given to the recently aggrandised Marquess of Winchester, William Paulet, who enjoyed the house, cloister and gardens for a while before ransacking most of what he found, stripping the lead off the roof timbers and demolishing most of the buildings.

The monuments, too, were sold off for a seemingly paltry £100, but the little chapel of the Friary fortunately remained more or less intact and in 1550 was given by Edward VI to London's growing population of refugees from Germany,

Denmark and the Netherlands. Soon known locally as the Dutch Church – at this time most Londoners didn't bother discriminating between one northern European and another – it survived the Great Fire but not the Blitz. Accordingly the pathway we see today runs alongside a 1957 rebuilding, but it would once have been the main access point to the original monastic buildings and burial ground.

Austin Friars, entered via a covered way from Throgmorton Street, twists and turns before giving on to Austin Friars Square. This almost certainly occupies the site of one of the old monastery courtyards, and while nothing of this remains – it's mostly Victorian now – the square itself retains some character with its old-fashioned lamps and ancient stone flags.

BACK ALLEY, EC3

Of no real interest, except as the last survivor of what must once have been hundreds of 'back alleys', this one originally gave on to the rear of the houses on Aldgate.

BAKERS' HALL COURT, EC3

Takes its name from the Worshipful Company whose hall is in nearby Harp Street. The present building forms part of an office development which dates back only to 1963, but the Bakers' Company can trace its roots back more than 850 years and received its royal charter in 1486. At that time only bakers of white bread were admitted to the livery, with bakers of brown bread forced to wait until 1569 – despite earlier attempts to merge the two – when they were happy to be admitted on an equal footing.

The Bakers' first hall in Harp Street was converted from the mansion of a fifteenth-century chamberlain, John Chichele, after the company acquired the building in 1506. This was rebuilt after the Great Fire, then again following another fire in 1715, and then once more when the eighteenth-century building was destroyed by enemy action in 1940.

BALL COURT, EC3

One of several charming little relics of eighteenth-century London, this tiny, narrow passage off Cornhill gives on to the wonderful bow-fronted Simpson's Tavern, a happy survivor of the many old London chophouses which used to throng this part of the City some 200 years ago. Completed in the late seventeenth century, though originally as a pair of dwellings, it was converted into a tavern in 1757 by a wine merchant and spirit seller called Tom Simpson and has no connection with the similarly named establishment on the Strand. Simpson ran the place himself until his death more than half a century later, then in 1808 his successor opened the restaurant where today diners still take pleasure in surroundings which struggle to avoid the description 'Dickensian' with their dark oak panelling, undecorated wooden tables and traditional English catering. There's even a rack for your black 'topper' or Muller Cut-down.

BARLEY MOW PASSAGE, EC1

Another alleyway taking its name from a popular public house, the first of which is known to have predated the existing building by at least 250 years. A covered, slightly claustrophobic passageway leading off Long Lane, while walking Barley Mow Passage it is still not hard to imagine the London of John Stow, author of *A Survey of London*. Observing in 1598 that the area was much built-up 'with tenements for brokers and tipplers and suchlike', he also recorded that 'the rest of Smithfield from Long Lane end to the bars is enclosed with inns and brewhouses'. Most, sadly, have now gone, including the Old Dick Whittington in John Betjeman's much-loved Cloth Fair. Often described as the oldest licensed premises in London – it was actually a seventeenth-century pub on fifteenth-century foundations – it was finally demolished in 1917.

BARTHOLOMEW PASSAGE, EC1

While the splendid gatehouse facing on to Little Britain is merely much-restored Tudor, St Bartholomew-the-Great is certainly the oldest church in the capital, the last surviving portion of an Augustinian priory founded in 1123 by Rahere, monk, prior and prebendary to St Paul's, and sometime *jongleur* or jester at the court of Henry I.

Today, as in previous centuries, it lies at the centre of a web of tiny thoroughfares. To several of these it has given its name, thus commemorating Rahere's famous promise when taken sick that he would build a hospital 'yn recreacion of poure men' if he was fortunate enough to recover. He did so – his hospital is modern day Bart's, of course – but his priory fared less well, although following its dissolution the central location and its undoubted utility meant some significant portions were spared the usual fate of being pulled down.

Sold to Sir Richard Rich once the monks had been expelled, the nave went but the choir survived and was used for storage and stabling for more than 300 years. Bloody Mary is said to have enjoyed concealing herself in the splendid gatehouse to watch the public executions which she herself had ordered, the gatehouse being later and beautifully restored by Sir Aston Webb (1849–1930).

Besides close associations with many of London's livery companies, St Bartholomew's still boasts the second oldest wooden door in London, five of its oldest bells, and the font in which William Hogarth was baptised in 1697. He was born in the Close which in 1725 was briefly home to Benjamin Franklin.

BATH COURT, EC1

It's hard to believe now, looking at this characterless corner of Roseberry Avenue, but this pleasant-sounding address owes its origins to Walter Baynes, a rich Inner Temple lawyer who acquired a series of fields here in 1697 with a view to developing them for housing. Finding one area to be frequently waterlogged, his investigations revealed a natural spring and he quickly amended his plans for the site. In the hope of persuading paying clients of the spring's health-giving properties, he set out to make a second fortune by building a bathhouse in what is now Coldbath Square.

Despite this decidedly unenticing name, the enterprise was soon up and running, described at the time as being 'in fine order for the reception of ladies and gentlemen' with the water 'serviceable to persons suffering from nervous disorders and dejected spirits'. On this basis it operated successfully for many years before, in 1794, giving its name to the Coldbath Fields Prison. Mentioned by Coleridge and Southey in *The Devil's Thoughts*, this was a house of correction, effectively a county gaol run by local magistrates with most inmates serving short sentences for minor crimes. It was, even so, on occasion used to house more serious felons, most pointedly those accused of playing a role in the celebrated Cato Street Conspiracy who were subsequently removed to the Tower and beheaded. By all accounts it was also more noted than most of its type for the severity of its regime, for the brutality of its warders, and for the use of a treadmill requiring prisoners to climb 8,640ft per six hours every day. It closed in 1877 and was finally torn down in 1889 with the old bath-house disappearing shortly afterwards. Today the Royal Mail's vast Mount Pleasant Sorting Office covers much of the site.

BEAR ALLEY, EC4

With bear-baiting rapidly becoming a popular pastime among Londoners after its arrival in Southwark from Italy in 1546, the Bear became a fashionable name for taverns. Prior to the Great Fire one such is known to have stood near this spot by the infamous River Fleet (named not for the speed of the flow, but from the Anglo-Saxon *fleot* meaning 'a place where boats floated'). It may well have been a popular venue during the heyday of what Pepys characterised as 'a very rude and nasty pleasure'.

Never one for rude pleasures, Cromwell tried to ban bear-baiting but failed, and it was not finally made illegal until 1835. Along with the bears the tavern too has gone. So too has most of the alley, having been amputated in 1869 to make way for the new Holborn Viaduct.

BEAR GARDENS, SE1

Although Italians are known to have put on a show for King John using imported bears out in Leicestershire, it wasn't until the mid-sixteenth century when the sport arrived in Bankside that it really began to pull in the punters.

For more than 120 years this stretch of the Thames offered the best spectacles, the most ferocious bears – each one primed by having their teeth filed down before they were tethered – and the biggest mastiffs, which were set loose from their kennels to tear and snap at the more or less defenceless beast. Rival entertainments started up near Clerkenwell Green and on Saffron Hill but eventually public tastes moved on.

Despite its great popularity, interest in the sport eventually began to dwindle. After visiting Bankside with friends in 1670, John Evelyn admitted that he too was 'heartily weary of this rude and dirty pastime' but it took until the 1830s before the sport was finally outlawed and the gardens closed for good.

BELL INN YARD, EC3

This commemorates a time when Leadenhall Market thrived and when Gracechurch Street thronged with at least a dozen taverns and galleried inns. Today just one survives, the New Moon, the fourteenth-century Bell Inn having reportedly commanded a rent of £3 per annum before falling to the Great Fire.

Afterwards it was not rebuilt, but the yard was reconstructed in a revised form as Bell Yard, and it remained more or less intact until the end of the nineteenth century when the expected commercial pressures were finally brought to bear. In 1933 during further redevelopment in neighbouring St Michael's Alley (see p. 166) excavations revealed a portion of Roman wall and a mass of old oyster shells indicating the presence of a Roman rubbish pit.

By this time the old houses had already been replaced by newer offices and today, if nothing else, it provides a convenient route through to St Michael Cornhill. In 1580 the church authorities here had to order everyone who kept chickens and hens in the churchyard to remove them, and eight years later – with parishioners still tending to look upon vestry land as their own – they were demanding that locals show some respect and cease hanging their laundry in the church precinct.

Today, with no such problems, it looks like the chaste, elegant Wren gem it is, with the Hawksmoor tower built after the style of his Magdalen College, Oxford, and its rare Renatus Harris organ – the one on which Henry Purcell once played. (And a very lucky survivor it is too, given that most of the seventeenth-century furniture and fittings were disposed of when the church was less than sensitively restored by Sir George Gilbert Scott in 1857.)

BENGAL COURT, EC3

Running off Birchin Lane (formerly Bechervereslane, a corruption of 'beard-carver' suggesting the presence of a barber or barbers in the area), at just 3 or 4ft wide Bengal Court is easy to miss and, like so many others, under repeated attack from developers. This charming backwater is at least 300 years old, however, and still connects with the small but characterful labyrinth of different alleyways and passages that cluster around Cornhill having been rebuilt after the disastrous fire of 1748. (This had been started accidentally by a maidservant at the Swan Tavern 'who left a candle burning in the shed'. Together with her name, more than a hundred buildings were lost to the flames which raged out of control for more than ten hours.)

Over the years Bengal Court has had several equally evocative aliases – including Sun Court, White Lion Alley and White Lion Court – with the present name dating only from 1906 but of uncertain derivation. Some small eighteenth-century properties survive along its north side, however, including the celebrated George & Vulture Tavern which retains its entrance in adjacent Castle Court (see p. 51).

BEVIS MARKS, EC3

A corruption of Berics or Bury's Marks, a reference to the London residence of the powerful abbots of Bury St Edmunds in Suffolk. Part of the boundary of the abbots' grounds would have been hereabouts, hence marks or markers. Today its most famous landmark is the Spanish and Portuguese Synagogue, the oldest Jewish place of worship in the country. The second to be established following the return of Jews after their expulsion by Edward I in 1290, it is a reminder that Britain's Jewish community has far deeper roots than is often imagined.

With the arrival of Cromwell – who reportedly used Jewish agents in important matters of state-endorsed espionage and diplomacy – Jews gradually began to return in substantial numbers and in 1701 a congregation of Sephardic Jews living around Creechurch Lane began looking to build in Bevis Marks.

Architecturally it differs little from many Christian churches of the period, indeed the building itself was erected by a Quaker master-builder. With one of the main roof support beams being presented to the community by Queen Anne, the elaborate chandeliers came from supporters in Amsterdam.

For more than 300 years many eminent Jews have worshipped here, among them Isaac D'Israeli. He was a devout member of the religious community and the birth of his son Benjamin is recorded in its archives. Others included Sir David Salomons (1797–1873) and Lionel de Rothschild, London's first Jewish Lord Mayor and Jewish MP respectively, although the law at that time (1851) prevented them from taking their seats and Salomons was fined £500 for speaking out of turn. He later removed the plaque at the base of the monument blaming Catholics for the Great Fire, and his nephew went on to organise the first-ever British motor show near his estate at Tunbridge Wells.

BISHOP'S COURT, EC4

Its name explained by its proximity to both St Paul's Cathedral and the site of the old Bishop's Head Tavern, the modern Court has little to recommend it besides the presence of the Magpie & Stump overlooking Old Bailey.

A former mughouse – drinking clubs so-called because the members kept their own vessels behind the bar – in the original Magpie & Stump drinks taken upstairs were traditionally charged at a higher price than those consumed below and for a singularly gruesome reason. Standing opposite the old Newgate Gaol, the remains of which have since 1907 been buried beneath the Central Criminal Court, customers would pay the extra for a grandstand seat upstairs in order to better see the public hangings. This centuries-old practice finally ceased on 26 May 1868 following London's last ever public execution – that of Fenian Michael Barrett who suffered the maximum penalty after blowing up seven people at Clerkenwell – a day on which it was reported, 'the Magpie and Stump did a roaring trade' and local householders were able to charge up to £10 for a ringside seat. More recently the pub has been reconstructed within a newer block, but it is still a favourite watering hole for lawyers so that one room is still known as Court No. 10 with Nos 1 to 9 being across the street.

BISHOP'S COURT, WC2

Sharing its fourteenth-century origins with nearby Lincoln's Inn and accessed from Chancery Lane, Bishop's Court would at one time have been the entrance to the townhouse of the bishops of Chichester. This was the property into which the lawyers moved in 1422, and which they purchased outright for £520 in 1580, thereby laying the ground for what became Lincoln's Inn.

The episcopal connection is commemorated not just by the name of the Court, but also in nearby Chichester Rents and indeed Chancery (or Chancellor) Lane, marking the fact that the most famous of the bishops, Ralph Neville, was appointed chancellor by Henry III.

The site fronting on to what had hitherto been called New Street had belonged to the king. But in 1227 he made it available to his new chancellor, agreeing that successive bishops would occupy the same office and enjoy the same considerable privileges.

This extraordinary settlement remained in place until 1340, after which the property passed into the hands of the Earls of Lincoln thereby providing one possible explanation for the name Lincoln's Inn. Further support for this theory comes from the lawyers' crest which includes a *lion rampant pupure* similar to that shown on Lord Lincoln's arms. Even so, it is not quite possible to discount a rival claim, namely the one made on behalf of Thomas de Lyncoln who, as the King's Serjeant of Holborn, clearly had equally strong local connections.

BLACKFRIARS COURT, EC4

Now just a short turn-in in front of one of London's most delightful and unusual pubs, Blackfriars Court for a long time extended some distance further north. Like the unique art nouveau pub, it took its name from the site it occupies, this having been home since the thirteenth century to the Dominican or Black Friars.

Moving from Chancery Lane in 1278, the monks built using even older materials salvaged from the Normans' Castle Baynard. Having played a role in the marital machinations of Henry VIII – their foundation was the venue for divorce proceedings against Catherine of Aragon – one is scarcely surprised to discover that at the Dissolution most of the buildings were torn down and their treasures carted off to the King's Jewel House.

That was in 1538; by 1597 the monks' refectory was being leased as a playhouse by Richard Burbage – Shakespeare, who lived in nearby Ireland Yard, was at one point his partner – and in the following century, after the theatre was closed by the Roundheads, it was demolished although a small portion of wall still survives in Playhouse Yard (see p. 144).

As a result, and in common with most monastic foundations built within the old City, almost nothing now remains of the structure. There are a few fragments of masonry in the aforementioned Ireland Yard, and some medieval stonework underpinning the walls of the seventeenth-century Apothecaries' Hall in Blackfriars Lane (which skirts the site of the old priory). In addition, a length of arcading was erected in Selsdon Park near Croydon after being uncovered in 1890, and part of the choir was similarly reused to build the new St Dominic's Priory on Haverstock Hill in 1925.

BLACKFRIARS PASSAGE, EC4

Becoming rich as a result of royal patronage, and vastly extending their property portfolio towards the end of the thirteenth century, the Black Friars were eventually able to construct a quay or wharf in 1294. By this time their lands extended as far as Bridewell and Puddle Dock, a small Thames inlet located to the east of the mouth of the River Fleet.

Running under the vast iron girders of Blackfriars railway bridge, the Passage passes beneath the station platforms before emerging opposite the former Mermaid Theatre which was built within the remains of a bombed-out warehouse. Here it meets the very unlovely Blackfriars Underpass, during the excavation of which in 1962 the remains of a wooden vessel were discovered.

The oldest of three boats discovered on this particular reach of the river, the so-called Blackfriars barge, a flat-bottomed, carvel-built vessel about 55ft long, is thought to have sunk at her moorings in about AD 150. Now displayed in the Museum of London, she was carrying Kentish ragstone up from the Medway, almost certainly for use in building the walls around the Roman City.

BLEEDING HEART YARD, EC1

Another pleasant cobbled yard named after a tavern, this particular one took its name from either an ancient Christian symbol or if you prefer (and many seem to) from an old and gruesome tale involving Lady Hatton, second wife of Sir William. A seventeenth-century society beauty, she is said to have paid the price after entering into a pact with the devil but then reneged on the terms. The organ in question was discovered the next morning (still pumping, of course, although her body was torn limb from limb) by a stable boy entering the yard. In an alternate version, her tryst was with Diego Sarmiento de Acuña, Conde de Gondomar, Spanish Ambassador to the Court of St James's from 1613 to 1622 – but perhaps it doesn't matter: the end result was much the same.

Much later Bleeding Heart Yard was to come to the attention of Charles Dickens. Fagin's den was nearby and in *Little Dorrit* the author gave a house in the yard to his Mr Plornish and built a workshop for Daniel Doyce. The place itself he described then as 'much changed in feature and in fortune, yet with some relish of ancient greatness about it'. You can see what he meant, even though the original tavern disappeared as long ago as 1785 – a new one was built in 1845 – when it and the yard were sold by the Hatton family at auction, as part of the anonymous-sounding 'Lot 71'.

BOLT COURT, EC4

For many years the Bolt-in-Tun Tavern stood nearby on the corner of Bouverie Street and Fleet Street until the site was completely built over in 1950. A coaching inn serving travellers to Lincoln and Cambridge, it had as its sign a crossbow bolt and a tun, in this case meaning a large cask that held two pipes, four hogsheads or 252 gallons of wine. While not perhaps a natural twosome their conjoining is far from unknown in London and appears elsewhere in the city, for example in an oriel window of the aforementioned church of St Bartholomew-the-Great. Here, as at the extraordinary Canonbury Tower in Islington, the symbol represents the rebus – the term is Latin for 'by things' and refers to a kind of word puzzle in which pictures are used to represent sounds – of William Bolton, Prior of St Bartholomew's during the reign of Henry VII.

Back to the court itself, which is where Dr Johnson came in 1776 and stayed until his death seven years later. Though these days associated more with Gough Square (see p. 96) where an earlier house of his is now a museum, Johnson moved into No. 8, a fairly small house which he filled with books and 'whole nests of people' who had come to depend on him for charity. It was here, too, that Boswell, having first met him in a bookshop, encountered Johnson for the very last time. The latter stepped down from a carriage at the entrance on Fleet Street and made with what Boswell called 'a kind of pathetic briskness' for his home down the dark alley after dining with the painter Reynolds. That was on 30 June 1784, Johnson dying the following December while Boswell was away in Scotland. The house itself burned down in 1819.

BOND COURT, EC4

Originally Bond's Court, after William Bond who was Alderman for the Walbrook Ward in 1649, although as late as 1792 *Kelly's Directory* still listed another William Bond, merchant, operating from No. 4. In fact, the Bond association with the ward seems to have been even more enduring than this, dating back to yet another William Bond, who was Sheriff of London in 1567, and to Alderman George Bond. From 1566 the latter lived in the magnificent Tudor Crosby Hall, the great Bishopsgate mansion – see Great St Helen's, p. 97 – which was removed brick by brick to Chelsea Embankment before the First World War but has more recently been reborn as London's largest private house.

BOTOLPH ALLEY, EC3

St Botolph (see Alderman's Walk, p. 15) was a seventh-century Saxon abbot who, as a travelling preacher, was eventually adopted as the patron saint of travellers. His home territory was East Anglia – Boston in Lincolnshire was formerly Botolph's Town – and he founded Icanhoh monastery, which is thought to have been at Iken, near Aldeburgh in Suffolk, before it was ransacked by the Danes.

With well over sixty different churches dedicated to him nationally – including the now ruined Augustinian priory at Colchester, unfortunately haunted by the town's drunks – four were also built within the City walls. St Botolph Billingsgate was destroyed in the Great Fire and never rebuilt, but St Botolph Aldersgate still survives along with St Botolph-without-Bishopsgate (where the poet Keats was baptised) and St Botolph's Aldgate. Each was built close to one of the old city gates leading the traveller to the world beyond.

Today the saint is commemorated by a row, a street, an alley and a lane (where Wren lived, and paid just £200 a year during the rebuilding of St Paul's) with this the most charming with its covered entrance, gas lanterns – now, alas, converted to low-energy bulbs – and traditional flagstone paving.

BOW CHURCHYARD, EC4

There have been churches on this site since before 1091, the year when the wooden roof of one of them is reported to have blown off in a storm and demolished an entire row of rude dwellings opposite. A couple of hundred years later disaster struck again, when the tower collapsed killing a score of worshippers: this was perhaps unsurprising since a fire had earlier been built at its base to smoke out an alleged murderer called William Fitz Osbert (see Bow Lane, below). Finally, in 1331, a wooden balcony collapsed during a jousting tournament, hurling Queen Philippa and her ladies-in-waiting to the ground – though fortunately without any fatal consequences.

The present church, however, dates back only to 1680 when (at a cost said to have exceeded that of any of his other fifty City churches) Sir Christopher Wren finished rebuilding the mighty church of St Mary-le-Bow. With its design based on the Roman Basilica of Maxentius, the name came from a series of brick arches in the original Norman crypt. What was at first St Mary de Arcubus – or 'St Mary of the Arches' – changed over time to 'of the Bows' to reflect the curvature of these ancient brick supports. Unfortunately, the churchyard had by that time more or less disappeared, with crooked developers in the area taking small bites out of it each time a building was replaced. Fortunately, a public-spirited citizen stepped in, a tailor called John Rotham who lived in an adjacent house, and gave what remained of his garden to create the small but welcome public space we see today.

BOW LANE, EC4

Pretty and twisted and a right of way for as long as 700 years, Bow Lane as such did not exist until the sixteenth century having previously been called Hosier Lane and, before that, Cordwainer Street after the hosiery, shoe- and bootmakers who at various times have set up their stalls here. The last of them left towards the end of Victoria's reign, but even now the narrow street and nearby Well Court and Groveland Court (see p. 105) are characterised by small retailers and cafés, their owners somehow clinging on despite a good deal of large-scale redevelopment surrounding what is now a Conservation Area.

Here in 1196 much excitement was caused when the afore-mentioned William Fitz Osbert, an erstwhile crusader known as Long Beard but identified by John Stow as 'a most seditious traitor', scaled the steeple of neighbouring St Mary-le-Bow and having 'fortified it with munitions and victualles' proceeded to wreak havoc. Eventually they smoked him out – almost wrecking the place in the process, so much for the ancient laws of sanctuary – and after being sent to the Tower he was dragged by his heels to Smithfield, executed and hanged in chains.

BREWHOUSE YARD, EC1

An obvious reference to London's many brewers who by the sixteenth century were active throughout the City – drawing water from the Thames, which is a worrying thought – with many more of them across the river in Southwark which enjoyed the benefit of slightly easier access to the hop fields of Kent. At this time most taverns would have brewed their own ales but the likelihood is that by the early eighteenth century a number of larger independent and commercial brewers were setting up shop in this part of the capital with the intention of servicing several taverns in their immediate locale. Certainly that was the case here, and indeed the giant Allied Brewers was still on site until quite recently, although by that time the yard had been reduced to the status of an office car park.

BRICK COURT, EC4

As with Stone House Court (see p. 190), so called because what were at first known as Brick Buildings were the first in the Middle Temple to be built of brick. Unfortunately, Nos 2–3 on the western side of the court were damaged beyond repair by enemy bombing in the 1940s.

Formerly housed in Wine Office Court (see p. 203), and ultimately buried on the north side of Temple Church, the Anglo-Irish writer and physician Oliver Goldsmith (1728–74) is the court's most famous resident. He wrote *She Stoops to Conquer* in a set of rooms he acquired here for £400 which were later occupied by William Thackeray.

BRIDE COURT, EC4

Originally called Green's Rents, the present name – first recorded in 1799 – comes from the adjacent 'journalists' church' of St Bride's, Fleet Street. The unusual dedication is to the fifth-century St Brigid of Kildare, a religiously inclined girl reputed to have been the daughter of an Irish prince and a druidic slave.

Evidence from excavations following an air raid in 1940 suggests that this part of the old City was home to a community of Irish settlers, but clearly at this time London would have attracted not just Celts but Angles and Saxons too, and indeed the same excavations uncovered Roman remains on the same site.

At least the eighth church to occupy this spot, the present building was built by Christopher Wren in 1703 to replace a previous building which had burnt down in 1666. By this time the church had acquired its own fire engine for just such an eventuality, but alas the wardens had failed to keep the machine 'scoured, oyled and trimmed' and it was of little use.

As a result, the destruction of the church was so complete that the worshippers couldn't even use the ruins temporarily (as happened elsewhere, including St Paul's). Today, despite destruction again raining down on the building in 1940, part of the medieval crypt of the pre-Wren church survives, its contents including more than 200 skeletons which – while not open to the public for inspection – have provided invaluable demographic intelligence about London's population in earlier times.

BRITTON'S COURT, EC4

With little if anything else to recommend it, Britton's Court is notable for the accidental discovery towards the end of the nineteenth century of a surviving fragment of a long-vanished Carmelite Priory which occupied this site between 1240 and the Dissolution. With everything above ground having disappeared long ago, what remains – fortunately on show behind plate glass in the basement of a modern block which is otherwise private – is a substantially intact crypt of rough chalk blocks with a ribbed ceiling and slightly domed roof.

Somewhat too small to have been of any importance when the priory was occupied by the White Friars – in 1895, being full of rubble and waste, it was mistaken by its discoverer for an old cellar – it is approximately 12ft square and in all likelihood provided nothing more than storage space and a discreet doorway out of the monastic precinct.

BRUNSWICK COURT, SE1

Now much reduced – it used to run all the way from Druid Street to Tanner Street – Brunswick Court appears to be gradually disappearing, not so much into the blackened railway arches but beneath successive waves of development around the environs of London Bridge station.

The name comes from a tavern, now gone, which used to serve those engaged in the Bermondsey Leather Market (hence nearby Tanner Street), Druid Street commemorating another public house, the Druid's Head or Tavern.

BUDGE ROW, EC4

Before reaching Soper Lane where it becomes part of the famous Roman Watling Street, Budge Row formed part of the medieval city's fur and skin trade. *Bogerow* being a reference to boge or budge furre, a type of lambskin, the Hall of the Worshipful Company of Skinners is nearby on Dowgate Hill.

Among the many City churches which have migrated – All Hallows Grass Church moved from Lombard Street to Twickenham; St Mary the Virgin, Aldermanbury, was rebuilt in Fulton, Missouri – the Row's parish church disappeared in 1875 before popping up in Peckham.

Dedicated to a celebrated hermit, and recognised as one of Wren's finest designs, St Antholin's was nevertheless knocked down to clear a path for the new Queen Victoria Street. The City paid for a new, far less distinguished St Antholin's in Nunhead Lane, Peckham – itself declared redundant in 2001.

The unwanted Wren spire, after being sold for just £5, was eventually installed as a rather sad piece of street sculpture in the midst of a 1960s housing estate in Sydenham. The church itself is pictured in relief on a memorial table on the side of St Mary Aldermary just off Bow Lane.

BULLS HEAD PASSAGE, EC3

For a long while something of an overspill area for stalls unable to squeeze into wonderful Leadenhall Market, a place of commerce funded in the 1440s through a legacy of Sir Richard Whittington. By the 1600s it was so successful that Dom Pedro de Ronquillo, Spain's Ambassador to the Court of St James's, told Charles II that more meat was sold there 'than in the whole of the Kingdom of Spain'.

Never more than a narrow alley, Bulls Head Passage quite appropriately therefore takes its name from a butcher's shop, a seventeenth-century tradesman whose shop was marked by a hanging sign depicting a bull's head. For a while the building (and the old sign) were given over to a Bull's Head Tavern, although neither survived into the twentieth century.

Incidentally, not everything brought to the market over the years has ended up being eaten: in 1835 a gander known as Tom was buried beneath the market having escaped the slaughterhouse axe and lived to the ripe old age of thirty-eight. A favourite with local stallholders and innkeepers, Tom was even accorded the unique honour of lying-in-state before being laid to rest.

BURY COURT, EC3

As at nearby Bury Street – and indeed that one's twin across London in St James's – the name references an old Suffolk connection. The two City addresses at the base of Ken Shuttleworth's almost instantly iconic 'hymn to the double-helix' at 30 St Mary Axe recall the powerful abbots of Bury St Edmunds who had a townhouse nearby, while the West End street is a development by Henry Jermyn, Earl of St Albans, whose country seat was outside the same town.

With the destruction of the abbey – one of Europe's largest – and the dispersal of its treasures, the abbots' London house passed to the Crown and thereafter to Sir Thomas Heneage. A royal chamberlain, Keeper of Records at the Tower, a Member of Parliament and reportedly one of Elizabeth's more favoured courtiers, Heneage unfortunately disregarded John Stow's glowing description – 'large of rooms, fair courts, and garden plots' – and had the great house pulled down so that the potentially valuable site could be developed by his descendants.

CAPEL COURT, EC2

Suffolk squire and Square Mile bigwig Sir William Capel, draper and twice Lord Mayor, in 1509 succeeded in raising the capital to build a small chapel on the south side of the church of St Bartholomew-by-the-Exchange. Six years later he was laid to rest here, together with Myles Coverdale (1488–1569), translator of the Bible into English. Unfortunately, both chapel and church – more commonly called Little St Bartholomew's to distinguish it from its more substantial rival at Smithfield – were destroyed in the Great Fire. Their replacements by Wren were then demolished in 1840 to make way for a rapidly expanding Bank of England.

CARDINAL CAP ALLEY, SE1

Barely a yard wide and inserted into a tiny terrace of pretty Georgian century houses, a plaque on one of which falsely asserts that Wren lived in it during the construction of St Paul's on the opposite side of the river. Lying in the shadow of Tate Modern, the name recalls the traditional scarlet *zucchetto* or skullcap worn by senior clerics, a Cardinal's Cap or Cardinal's Hat Tavern is known to have existed here before the year of the Armada. It is not known which cardinal if any it referred to, however, although much of the land and property in this area was in the possession of the abbots of St Mary Overie (now Southwark Cathedral) and later of the bishops of Winchester until the Dissolution.

CARTER LANE, EC4

A blue plaque commemorates the site of the once mighty Blackfriars Priory in what was presumably a convenient if meandering cut-through for working carters and carmen wishing to avoid the slow-wheeled traffic on Ludgate Hill. It is a happy survivor; throughout the 1970s it looked likely to be destroyed in a City scheme to drive a new street through the area to the south of St Paul's.

Besides the many small but delightful thoroughfares which run off it, such as Wardrobe Place and Cobb's Court, it is notable for the extraordinary, late nineteenth-century building on the corner with Dean's Court. An Italianate building with Renaissance sgraffito decoration, this is the most recent building to occupy a site which from the early seventh century until our own was home to the St Paul's Cathedral Choir School. More recently the school switched to become co-educational and moved to New Change, and the vacant building with its vibrant façade, slightly weird ecclesiastical symbols and Latin inscriptions has been reborn as a Youth Hostel.

CASTLE COURT, EC3

One of the most rewarding areas to explore in the City is the veritable maze of little alleys, footpaths and courtyards clustered around Cornhill. One of the best known is Castle Court thanks to the George & Vulture, a historic chop-house. Its clientele is said to have included the brilliant Robert Hooke and Charles Dickens – Mr Pickwick lunches Sam Weller here in the eponymous *Papers* – and, less credibly, Geoffrey Chaucer and Dick Whittington.

Even without these two unlikely patrons, however, it's a special place. Distinguished by the ghost of a grey lady in the upstairs dining room and by a couple of parish markers – the boundary between St Michael Cornhill and St Edmund the King, Lombard Street, actually bisects the main restaurant – it also has a wonderfully colourful tale to explain the name.

For many years it was simply called the George until a City vintner moved into a nearby building. He had a tethered live vulture outside in place of a more traditional hanging sign, and when he moved on, the tavern – which post-Fire had served as a temporary office – adopted the bird as its own.

Like so many establishments in London it is said to have been a regular haunt of the legendary Hellfire Club. More certain is that since 1950 it has hosted the Dickens Pickwick Club as well as an annual dinner for descendants of the author.

CATHERINE WHEEL ALLEY, E1

While the Puritans, unhappy with any reference to Catholic martyrs, frequently insisted on a name change to the otherwise meaningless 'Cat and Wheel', the Catherine Wheel was a popular name for taverns in and around London. One such – a galleried coaching inn – stood here until 1901, when it was torn down following a disastrous fire. The largely modern developments which line the alleyway mean there is little of interest here today besides some outstanding graffiti and the sad tale of Dirty Dick, after whom another local pub is named.

Generally assumed to be a reference to Dick Turpin, the celebrated Essex highwayman, the Dick in question is actually Nathaniel 'Dick' Bentley who lived and worked in nearby Leadenhall Street. A wealthy, well-known and fashionably attired City trader, Bentley became distressed by the death of his fiancée in 1804 and, refusing to wash or mend his clothes, adopted an increasingly reclusive way of life for his remaining years.

When he died five years later, something of a local celebrity, the landlord of the Old Jerusalem acquired Bentley's meagre possessions – including a dead cat and countless cobwebs – and put them on display in his cellar. The pub soon became known

to all as Dirty Dick's and eventually changed its name. Poor old Nathaniel also providing the inspiration for Charles Dickens when he came to describe the wealthy spinster Miss Havisham in his novel *Great Expectations*.

CAVENDISH COURT, EC2

Like nearby Devonshire Square, where the Cavendish earls (now dukes) of Devonshire kept a house until the 1670s, the name commemorates one of the country's great landowning families although the house itself had actually been built not for them but for Jasper Fisher, a City goldsmith.

Constructed on a vast scale and surrounded by substantial gardens, the project nearly bankrupted its wealthy owner and by the time it was taken over by Sir Roger Manners, an Elizabethan courtier, it had become known locally as 'Fisher's Folly'. Subsequently it was owned by the earls of Oxford and of Argyll before Lord Devonshire acquired it. By 1666 he had let part of it to a Quaker community – one preacher would arrive wearing a nightcap in the sure knowledge that he would be carted off to spend another night in the cells – and a decade later sold it to the developer Nicholas Barbon (*c.* 1640–98), sometime owner of Osterley House.

The son of 'Praise God' Barbon – a celebrated sectarian, he'd actually been christened Unless-Jesus-Christ-Had-Died-For-Thee-Thou-Hadst-Been-Damned Barbon – Barbon Jr was later to move on to greener pastures outside the City where he was one of the prime movers in the creation of the aristocratic quarter which would become known as the West End. Here, for the time being, he contented himself with pulling down the great mansion and building on its foundations.

Today its precise location can be gauged by the knowledge that this little court would once have provided access for tradesmen and the owner's servants.

CHANGE ALLEY, EC3

Originally Exchange Alley after the nearby Royal Exchange, until the aforementioned Cornhill fire of 1748 the street was home to a number of fashionable coffee houses, most notably Jonathan's and Garraway's both of which are accorded plaques, although the dates on these are not accurate.

Today the former is best known for its involvement in the South Sea Bubble fiasco: as a place where speculators could meet to buy and sell, its customers witnessed the ruination of many in 1720 when shares tumbled from around £1,200 to just £150. In July 1772 *The Gentleman's Magazine* reported that its informal role was now to be formalised and that 'it should be called the Stock Exchange, which is to be wrote over the door' – and so it was until a move took place to larger premises in nearby Threadneedle Street.

While the stockbrokers and jobbers favoured Jonathan's, Garraway's reputation was more as an informal auction house. As well as being somewhere to sell war booty, it was early on associated with the Hudson's Bay Company, selling furs in the late 1660s before moving on to sugar, coffee, spices and salvaged goods. By 1670 tea was selling here at an incredible £10 a pound, Thomas Garraway himself promoting the new beverage as 'the cure for all disorders' and selling it alongside his famous cherry wine and punch.

Both places were rebuilt after the Great Fire – one lot consigned for auction at Garraway's comprised 'one box of chocolate,

46 bags of snuff and an elephant tooth' – but neither was ever quite the same.

Jonathan's finally closed for good in 1866, and in 1872 Garraway's was knocked down to make way for a branch of Martin's Bank which has since been absorbed into Lloyds Banking Group. Since then, of course, and not without irony, many of the banks, insurance offices and other financial institutions which replaced the coffee houses have now themselves been converted into places where one can unwind over a drink. A third blue plaque nearby marks the site of the King's Arms Tavern 'where the first meeting of the Marine Society was held on 25 June 1756'.

CHARTERHOUSE SQUARE, EC1

Not square at all but, still cobbled and gated, the architectural variety of Charterhouse Square and pretty Charterhouse Mews encompasses the elegant curved 1930s façade of Guy Morgan's Florin Court as well as the gatehouse of the seventeenth-century Sutton's Hospital which was founded at a cost of £13,000 to educate forty-four poor boys and house eighty poor gentlemen.

Also known as the Charterhouse, after the Carthusian monastery which occupied the site from the fourteenth century, the establishment was the gift of Thomas Sutton, thought in 1611 to be 'the richest commoner in England'. In 1872 the boys departed when the school, still known as Charterhouse, relocated to Godalming in Surrey. Thereafter, albeit briefly, the buildings were occupied by another venerable educational establishment, the Merchant Taylors' School, but today – in those portions which survived the wartime bombing – only the poor gentlemen remain.

In what is essentially a retirement home, they are quirkily if not quite fairly described as 'decrepit Captaynes either at Sea or Land, and Souldiers maymed or ympotent'. Around the corner is a pub, the Sutton Arms, and nearby Dallington Street shares the same association being named after one of the almshouse's early masters. The author and traveller Sir Robert Dallington (1561–1637) was a generous benefactor to his home village of Geddington in Northamptonshire, as well as a Gentleman of the Bedchamber to Charles I.

CHURCH COURT, EC4

Growing out of the Cloister Court and so named for the historic Temple Church which, while subjected to so many restorations over the centuries that 'every ancient surface was repaired away or renewed', still follows the same basic twelfth-century ground plan that was said to have been modelled on Jerusalem's Church of the Holy Sepulchre. Consecrated on 10 February 1185 during a visit to London by Heraclius, Patriarch of Jerusalem, the tranquillity and atmosphere of the ancient church is still coming under assault from credulous fans of *The Da Vinci Code* in which it played a minor role.

CHURCH ENTRY, EC4

The church in question is the sixteenth-century St Ann's, built on land belonging to the Black Friars and later amalgamated with St Andrew-by-the-Wardrobe rather than being rebuilt after the Great Fire. Unfortunately that too was destroyed by fire, in the 1940 Blitz. Today its graveyard is a small paved garden, a plaque nearby commemorating the great Dominican Priory and recording that 'on this plot of land stood, in the Middle Ages, part of the Provincial's hall of the Dominican Priors of Blackfriars with the dorter over' – while noting that the last burial was made here in 1849. Note too the entrance to the Vestry Hall, the work of Fletcher Bannister, author of the invaluable, multi-edition *History of Architecture.*

CLEARY GARDEN, EC4

Named after Fred Cleary (1905–84), a member of the Court of Common Council between 1959 and 1984 and a campaigner for the preservation and expansion of public space in the Square Mile. Cleary Garden faces on to busy Queen Victoria Street but manages somehow to be both peaceful and secluded.

Like many such open spaces, Cleary Garden itself is a direct result of enemy action. The area was cleared of bomb-damaged buildings following the Second World War and set aside as a terraced garden after workers engaged in the demolition work uncovered the remains of two Roman baths. Today its green terraces and rose- and vine-hung trellises provide a wonderfully shady enclave for City workers (or visitors to Tate Modern or the College of Arms), the whole having been relandscaped in 2007 to become the Loire Valley Wines Legacy Garden. With aromatic plantings to evoke the flavours and bouquet of wines from that region, the association is not quite as bizarre as it sounds, as the site was used throughout the Middle Ages by London vintners as a place to trade wines imported from France.

CLEMENT'S INN PASSAGE, WC2

Today London's historic legal enclaves comprise just four Inns of Court – Lincoln's, Gray's, Middle and Inner Temple – but originally these institutions were far more numerous. Formerly known as the Inns of Chancery, a name denoting their original role in training the chancery clerks charged with preparing the writs in the medieval kings' courts, their number once included many smaller entities. These included Barnard's Inn, Clement's, Clifford's (see overleaf), Furnival's, Lyon's, New and Staple Inn before a slow process of consolidation in the 1530s resulted in the big four taking control of and eventually closing the remainder.

Adjacent to the Royal Courts of Justice, Clement's Inn functioned as a sort of hostel for young men training for a career in the law and was so named, observed John Stow in 1598, 'because it standeth near to Clement's Church, but nearer to the fair fountain called Clement's Well'. On the parish boundary, an old iron marker set into the paving marks the position where the well once stood.

The Inn itself was small, occupying just three courtyards and a hall, but is distinguished from its rivals by a mention in Shakespeare with a justice in the second act of *Henry IV* declaring that 'he must to the Inns of Court. I was of Clement's once myself, where they talk of Mad Shallow still.' Unfortunately, even such fame as this was not enough to protect it from demolition in 1891, but one painting from the hall has survived and now hangs in the hall of the Inner Temple while a small Italian sundial from one of the courts has also been re-erected following its purchase from the lawyers for 20 guineas.

CLIFFORD'S INN PASSAGE, EC4

The fate of Clifford's Inn was broadly similar, Robert, 3rd Baron de Clifford having occupied a house and some land here in 1307 and his widow leasing it to a group of lawyers for £10 a year in 1343. Eventually the lawyers were able to acquire the freehold, and thereafter it continued to function as an Inn of Chancery for some five and a half centuries.

Its most notable pupil was perhaps Norfolk landowner and jurist Sir Edward Coke (1552–1634) who prosecuted both Sir Walter Raleigh and the Gunpowder Plotters. He was also the first to observe that an Englishman's home is his castle – noting in 1604 that 'the house of every one is to him as his castle and fortress, as well for his defence against injury and violence as for his repose' thereby establishing in law the principle of freedom from arbitrary search and seizure.

In 1903 his successors, the 'Rules' or senior members, managed to sell the site for £100,000 to a builder called William Willet. Hoping to keep what they could by no means have earned in this way, the lawyers were eventually, fortunately, required instead to set aside most of the sum to promote legal education through the office of the Attorney General for England and Wales.

When Willet's plans for the site fell through the premises were occupied by the Society of Knights Bachelor – Leonard and Virginia Woolf were briefly tenants, the latter making her first attempt at suicide while living here – but in 1934 the remaining buildings were demolished, leaving only this narrow passage leading from Fleet Street to the inn's former gatehouse, which still survives.

CLOTH FAIR, EC1

For centuries home to drapers and cloth merchants (including the father of architect Inigo Jones) and later Sir John Betjeman at No. 43, the cloth fair in question was the famous Bartholomew Fair which was held at Smithfield late each summer. It thrived from 1133 to 1855 when it was suppressed by the City authorities on the grounds that – like the May Fair and Southwark's Lady Fair before it – the event had started to encourage debauchery and an unacceptable level of public disorder.

Architecturally the house at Nos 41–42 is a nice essay in the transition from timber to brick building in the area and as such provides a tantalising glimpse of old London. It was completed in about 1615 using both materials while its neighbours appear more conventionally Georgian with new regulations following the Great Fire having made it more difficult to build with wood. Otherwise a depressing loss in the area was the demolition in 1915 of another row of houses backing on to the churchyard of St Bartholomew-the-Great.

Dismissed by the writer and raconteur Augustus Hare (1834–1903) as 'old though squalid houses of Elizabethan and Jacobin date', these were important survivors of the medieval street pattern. Unfortunately with their picturesque hanging storeys and internal courtyards, they were torn down despite remonstrations from many leading antiquarians.

COOPER'S ROW, EC3

Leading off one corner of Trinity Square, just by Tower Hill station, the best feature of Cooper's Row is also by far the oldest, namely a substantial portion of the original Roman city wall which was constructed between AD 190 and 220 and survived long enough to be incorporated into a block of warehouses in the nineteenth century. A singularly impressive piece of work, particularly if viewed from the outside, today the wall is best viewed from the station exit. Here a stretch around 100ft long reaches a height of around 35ft – the lower courses Roman work, the remainder 'new' (i.e. medieval) – a lucky survivor of the 1766 ruling from the City authorities that anyone wishing to remove stone from the wall for their own purposes was free to do so. In this way an estimated 1 million cubic feet of stone were removed and reused and the wall largely lost for good.

CORBET COURT, EC3

Private property, a frequent haunt of wheel-clampers and so by no means easy to access, this may once have been named Corbett's Court after a seventeenth-century builder and developer who attempted what has now been achieved, namely shutting off what was once a public right of way. A carved stone representation of the Mercers' Maiden – the capital's oldest – provides an indication as to the historical owners, her likeness being seen around the City and as far west as Covent Garden.

COWPER'S COURT, EC3

John Cowper was a sixteenth-century City alderman who lived nearby and in the early 1900s builders uncovered a series of brick vaults believed to have been part of the cellars of his house. He died in 1609 and was buried in nearby St Michael Cornhill. The name also recalls one of his descendants, the poet and satirist William Cowper (1731–1800) who died of dropsy after many years as a victim of depression.

In the 1840s the court was home to the Jerusalem Coffee House. Despite its name this was popular among India, Far East and China merchants as a place to do business and to hear the latest trading news. Later traders with Australia joined them and by 1879 with 300 to 400 subscribing members what had by now formally become the Jerusalem Exchange moved to Billiter Street and the old eighteenth-century premises were converted to offices.

CRANE COURT, EC4

An L-shaped thoroughfare joining Fetter Lane and Fleet Street, Crane Court deserves to be better known than it is, having played a role in the cultural history of England, completely at odds to its appearance and modest proportions.

First mentioned in 1662, shortly before it was razed and rebuilt following the Great Fire, the place took its name from a nearby tavern, the Two Cranes, and in the early eighteenth century was home to Sir Edward Browne, President of the (not-yet Royal) College of Physicians. In 1710 Sir Edward's residence was sold to the prominent gentlemen comprising 'a Colledge for the Promoting of Physico-Mathematicall Experimentall

Learning' – today's august Royal Society – whose members moved from Sir Thomas Gresham's old Bishopsgate mansion, the site of which is now occupied by the City's dominating Tower 42.

Thereafter the Royal Society met here in Crane Court for more than seventy years, eventually removing to more commodious rooms in Somerset House – in 1782 Sir Edward's old house was sold for a useful £1,000 – and doing so despite having numbered among its membership several individuals (most obviously Wren, Hooke and Evelyn) who might have designed from scratch something rather better.

Described at the time as 'neither large nor handsome', the Fellows' house at Crane Court was nevertheless more spacious than Bishopsgate had been, and included behind it room for a small museum. Here the exhibits, according to a contemporary catalogue, included such wonderful curiosities as 'a flying squirrel, which for a good nut-tree will pass a river on the bark of a tree, erecting his tail for a sail; the leg-bone of an elephant; a bone said to be taken out of a mermaid's head; and a mountain cabbage – one reported 300 feet high.'

Arguably even less concerned with accuracy than the compiler of said catalogue – the elephant bone had been mistaken for that of a giant – Crane Court's other residents at this time included various printers and publishers keen to avoid paying the government stamp or tax then due on all publications. To this end, reported *The Bookseller*, 'various ingenious devices were employed to deceive and mislead the officers employed by the Government'. These included the ostentatious distribution around nearby streets of decoy parcels, typically comprising waste or even blank paper, while the genuine article was quietly slipped out through the back door.

While its proximity to Fleet Street made it an obvious place for such subterfuge, a few more legitimate publications were eventually able to claim a connection with Crane Court, too. In a series of rooms at No. 9, for example, the very first editions of *Punch* were put together, while another similarly long-lived weekly – *The Illustrated London News* – began life at No. 10. Two other houses have less happy associations, however: those at Nos 5 and 6 were badly damaged by a fire in 1971 after having been identified as the very oldest houses in London to have been built by the prominent post-Fire speculator and developer Nicholas Barbon.

CRAWFORD PASSAGE, EC1

Not infrequently the colourful tales associated with London's backwaters turn out to have as much truth as fiction – but not, I fear, in the case of Crawford Passage. The story goes that there once stood here a tavern known as the Pickled Egg, and indeed writing his *Old and New London* in 1878 Thornbury confirms that the passage was for a long time known as Pickled Egg Walk. Apparently the pub was so called because it was the very first in London to sell pickled eggs, the originals having been introduced to the capital by 'a Dorsetshire or Hampshire man, who here introduced to his customers a local delicacy'.

So far so believable, at least until the introduction to the narrative of a wandering Charles II. Travelling with Nell Gwyn – who else? – Thornbury suggests that His Majesty 'during one of his suburban journeys, once stopped here to taste a pickled egg, which is said to be a good companion to cold meat'. Apparently the pair had been fishing nearby on the shaded upper reaches of the River Fleet, in reality a watercourse which was already a notorious sewer, but suddenly feeling hungry they dropped into the nearby tavern for a bite to eat. In their honour the place was hastily renamed, and with it the alleyway outside, only for the next publican to rename it again – after himself, he hated pickled eggs – as Crawford's Tavern.

CROWN COURT, EC4

Leaving aside the Crown Court, the place where barristers line their pockets and villains get sent down, the capital's overabundance of Crown courts, yards, streets, passages, alleyways, lanes and mews are more often associated with similarly named inns and taverns than the monarch. Here, however, there is one of those rare, royal connections.

Situated just off ancient Cheapside this particular Crown Court would have been close to the now long-vanished Crown Fields, a tilt yard or jousting arena which lay to the east of the great church of St Mary-le-Bow. Especially popular with Edward II, Crown Fields eventually came to include an unusually substantial stone grandstand built on the orders of the king who, records Stow, assembled with his entourage 'there to behold the joustings and other shows at their pleasure'. Unfortunately the structure – which Stow calls a shed – was so large as to 'greatly darkeneth the said church' but the king was determined it should be built having personally witnessed the collapse of an earlier wooden stand or balcony and the injuries which resulted on that occasion.

By 1410 the new and improved 'shed' had nevertheless lost some of its original purpose and so was conveyed by Henry IV to a partnership of local merchants for use as a market when no jousting was taking place. Cheapside, *chepe* meaning market, had by this time long been a place renowned more for retail than entertainment, and today the modern Crown Court occupies the site of the king's private entrance gate into the aforementioned Crown Fields.

CROWN OFFICE ROW, EC4

The original Crown Office was a Tudor administration responsible for the issuance of bills of indictment, an arrangement which pertained until 1621 when it was removed to King's Bench Walk (p. 119) and later still to the Royal Courts in the Strand. The Row itself was subsequently rebuilt by Sir Sidney Smirke (1798–1877), the north country architect responsible for the Reading Room at the British Museum, the remodelling of Burlington House for the Royal Academy, the Imperial War Museum and the original Pall Mall premises of the Carlton Club. In the 1950s it was rebuilt again, however, this time by Sir Edward Maufe, although a plaque indicates where in the older building – at No. 2 – Charles Lamb had been born in 1775.

After being called to the Bar in 1848, Thackeray took chambers here, at No. 10, which he shared with the editor of *Punch*, Tom Taylor. Describing the rooms years later, Taylor recalled them as 'fusty, they were musty, they were grimy, dull, and dim, the paint scaled off the panelling, the stairs were all untrim; the flooring creaked, the windows gaped, doorposts stood awry, the wind whipt round the corner with a wild and wailing cry'.

DEAN'S COURT, EC4

Constructed in 1670, Dean's Court, specifically what is now the Old Deanery, was the official residence of the Dean of St Paul's, the individual appointed by the Crown and (together with the Chapter or canons) responsible for the administration and fabric of the cathedral as well as deciding who is afforded the privilege of a baptism, marriage and indeed burial within the precincts of the building.

For such an important figure one is perhaps not surprised to discover that the Deanery was designed and built by none other than Sir Christopher Wren. It is indeed an exceptionally grand, redbrick house, vaguely Dutch in tone and standing behind a tall curtain wall unexpectedly secluded given its central position.

For a long time used as commercial premises (but in the 1990s returned to domestic usage) the Court was also occupied by lesser officials employed by the Vicar General and in the consistory courts. Another judicial entity, the confusingly named House of Doctors – otherwise Doctors' Commons or the Court of Civilians – occupied a site on the east side from 1532.

Here in the quaintly titled Courts of Arches, Admiralty, Delegates, Prerogatives, Faculty and Archdeacons, battalions of lawyers presided over slow, costly proceedings in a manner described by Charles Dickens as 'a cosey, dosey, old-fashioned, time-forgotten, sleepy-headed little family party'. He also accused them of playing 'all kinds of tricks with obsolete old monsters of Acts of Parliament' so it was perhaps little wonder that a drive for greater efficiency caused them to be amalgamated with the High Court in 1857 and shortly thereafter dissolved.

DEVEREUX COURT, WC2

Named after Robert Devereux, Earl of Essex, whose townhouse was acquired in the 1670s and demolished by the prolific seventeenth-century developer Nicholas Barbon responsible for nearby Essex Street and Essex Court. A bust of Devereux looks down from the wall of the Devereux, until 1843 the Grecian Coffee House and now a pub. Together with Nos 23 and 24 it is a genuine Barbon survivor, dated 1676 although it was substantially modified in the following century.

DEVONSHIRE ROW, EC2

Originally a through-way into Devonshire Square, and so a reference to the sixteenth-century townhouse of a family of territorial magnates, the Cavendishes, at the time the Earls and now Dukes of Devonshire. Bought advantageously from a bankrupt goldsmith and Clerk to the Court of Chancery (Jasper Fisher, see Cavendish Court, p. 54), the Devonshires' establishment was soon sufficiently grand that the 3rd Earl's countess was able to entertain Charles II here. Outside, the forecourt was of such a scale that, when the house eventually went, the carriage drive was transformed into the aforementioned Devonshire Square.

The likes of the Cavendish family were relatively rare in the City, patrician and noble families tending mostly to prefer London's relatively new 'West End'. They lingered here longer than most rich families too, and into the mid-seventeenth century Christian, dowager countess of Devonshire, could still be seen on most afternoons emerging into the bustle of the commercial city, her gilded coach accompanied by her chaplain, her doctor, her chief steward and several footmen. Upon her return home she would be met by twelve women waiting either side of the steps up to the house.

Eventually this anachronism was brought to a halt, however, whereupon the destruction of yet another great City mansion fell to the developer Barbon. He had purchased the property in 1675 from the 4th Earl (subsequently 1st Duke) and quickly set to profit from the site by rebuilding. Today, as a result, perhaps the best thing about the Row is nearby Cutler's Gardens and the other restored eighteenth-century warehouses in and around New Street and Cock Hill where a splendid stone gateway survives. Built between 1770 and 1820 for the Honourable East India Company, and more recently landscaped by garden designer Russell Page, the complex changed hands for more than £400 million in 2006 since when on-site security men have been more than usually keen to tell visitors to put away their cameras.

One other good thing is the Bull Inn, which in one form or another has been standing in Devonshire Row for some 400 years. Local legend has it that Thomas Hobson, the Cambridge carrier who used to rent out horses to the London mails, used to drink here occasionally. Rather than allowing customers to pick a horse he sent them out in strict rotation in order that the older nags wouldn't be worn out – a sensible if inflexible system from which we get the saying 'Hobson's Choice', denoting an apparent choice which on closer examination is no choice at all.

DOBY COURT, EC4

From the thirteenth century the area was called Maidenhead Court because it ran off Maiden Lane. It became Doby Court in about 1800 when the latter was renamed Skinners Lane, after the premises of the Worshipful Company of Skinners on nearby Dowgate Hill. Who Doby was is still unclear, although the likelihood is that a Mr Doby owned some properties here. Much developed (although the original cobbles have happily survived), Doby Court is also now somewhat truncated, having for a long time extended further north to a narrow covered passageway out into Queen Street.

DORSET BUILDINGS, EC4

Following the Reformation, which saw the Bishops of Salisbury deprived of their London mansion, considerable property in the vicinity came into the possession of the Sackville family, future Earls of Dorset. Promptly renamed Dorset House, the bishops' mansion and gardens occupied a substantial corner of the City, an area now covered by Dorset Buildings, Dorset Rise, Salisbury Square and Salisbury Court (p. 175) with gardens running down to the Thames.

The house itself fell to the flames in September 1666, though reportedly when the Great Fire was still almost half a mile distant. For a while it looked as though it might be saved, when the Duke of York's bargemaster saw flames leaping from the tiles and called for help. Unfortunately the fire was soon too fierce to fight, and the troops withdrew, leaving the house to its fate.

The Earl then let out the 'stables and out howses towards the water side … to make a playhouse for the children of the revels,' and in 1671 Wren built them a new theatre on the site. Called the Dorset House Theatre, and said to have cost £9,000, it was large enough to seat 1,000 and sufficiently grand to become the chief theatre in London when the Theatre Royal in Drury Lane burned down a year later. However, renamed the Queen's, it eventually fell from favour, becoming a somewhat less elegant venue for wrestlers and pugilists, before finally being demolished in 1709. It was later replaced by a timber wharf and, later still, the yard for the City of London School.

DRAPERS' GARDENS, EC2

While many of those livery companies which are lucky enough to still have their own halls continue to own and control a considerable acreage within the Square Mile, most of their gardens have long since disappeared. Some have courtyards – favourites include the Apothecaries' and the Haberdashers' – and in the shadow of 140 London Wall (designed by the creators of the famous 'Skylon' at the Festival of Britain) the herb garden attached to Barber-Surgeons' Hall is an unexpected pleasure.

Once dozens of livery companies boasted similar spaces of their own – some large enough to have bowling alleys and even banqueting houses – although today most are now commemorated only by name.

At least here in Drapers' Gardens a very small portion of the original garden survives, a compact courtyard last rebuilt in 1869 by Herbert Williams. With sculptures by Edward Wyon, and some mulberry trees planted by the Queen in 1955 and the

Prince of Wales in 1971, it is certainly attractive. There is even so nothing to match the days when the company's garden would have produced all the herbs and flowers for official banquets, and when there was space left, for the warden's gardener to plant the borders with herbs and vegetables for his master's private profit.

During the Tudor and Stuart periods such places would have been about prestige as well as productivity, and liverymen of all companies would have been keen to see the gardens in tip-top condition for their important ceremonial occasions. Accordingly, the Drapers employed a full-time gardener, while on London Wall the Carpenters' Company allowed 7s a year for the Beadle's wife to weed the garden and 2s a day (plus drink) for outside gardeners to be brought in for special occasions. Similarly meticulous accounts show the Grocers to have spent £44 2s 5d in 1589/90 on 106 loads of dung, 42 loads of gravel, and the plants needed for a major horticultural refurbishment.

Today, even with all this kind of thing swept away long ago, Drapers' Gardens nevertheless still manages to exude a pleasant air of the past, and does so despite finding itself surrounded by veritable canyons of high-rise office developments. In part this is because one side is effectively protected from any serious development by Drapers' Hall itself. The Hall's history goes back to 1530, although the company can trace its own history back to the twelfth century.

The plot had originally been owned, or at least occupied, by Thomas Cromwell, variously the Master of the King's Jewels, Lord Privy Seal, Vicar General and Earl of Essex. Needing a residence worthy of his growing status, Cromwell seems to have sequestrated the property of several smaller men, including the father of London's great chronicler John Stow who was forced to surrender his garden to Cromwell's greedy machinations.

According to Stow, 'no man durst go to argue the matter, but each man lost his land' but happily, in time, Cromwell lost his head (after picking a quarrel with Henry VIII) and in 1541 his house was purchased by the Drapers' Company for their own use. By 1607 they sounded almost as grand as Cromwell, having that year been reincorporated as 'The Masters and Wardens and Brethren and Sisters of the Guild or Fraternity of Blessed Mary the Virgin of the Mystery of Drapers of the City of London'. But looking around Drapers' Gardens 400 years later, it seems fair to say that as landowners they have proved to be better neighbours than the reviled Cromwell.

DUNSTER COURT, EC3

In London in the Middle Ages there were a number of guilds and fraternities associated with the cloth trade, two of which – the Fullers and the Shearmen – combined in 1528 to form the last of the 'Great Twelve' liveries, today's Worshipful Company of Clothworkers. Among those to sign the first ordinances was Sir Thomas More. When he visited the hall many years later, Samuel Pepys found the 'entertainment very good. Good company and very good Musique.'

As the Guild or Fraternity of the Assumption of the Blessed Virgin Mary of Clothworkers in the City of London, the members found they preferred the hall of the Shearmen to that of the Fullers and moved in. Accordingly they can claim to have occupied this site just off Mincing Lane since the 1450s although the present building was completed as recently as 1958. Sharing the usual fate for such structures, its predecessors were twice destroyed – in the Great Fire, and then the Blitz – with a third having to be dismantled in 1855 after its foundations proved unequal to the task asked of them.

That first hall inherited by the new body in 1528 had been built on a site granted between 1170 and 1197 by Prior Stephen of Holy Trinity Priory, Aldgate, to a local tiler and builder. It was later conveyed to the Shearmen in 1456, at which time Dunster Court was more commonly called Dunstan's after the saint.

By 1548, however, the liverymen had outgrown the hall and commissioned a new building from Henry Davyson, bricklayer, and John Sampson, carpenter. Considerably larger than the first, and perhaps the most picturesque of the six built to date, it included separate chambers for ladies as well as a counting house, armoury and a knot garden planted with sweet-smelling lavender, rosemary, thyme and hyssop as well as vines.

Today, like so many, the garden is gone, and the present, modest neo-Georgian Hall dramatically overshadowed by Minster Court, aka Monster Court or Batman's Castle, which was described by one observer as a 'flagrantly populist pile of peaks and gables … like Hanseatic Gothic done in stiff folded paper'. To compensate for this modish horror the entrance to the court at least has a large pair of more traditional wrought-iron gates beneath the arms of the Clothworkers complete with two stone griffin supporters.

EAGLE COURT, EC1

With such a majestic bird in the name, the obvious conclusion would be that hereabouts, at some time, there stood a tavern named after Britain's most impressive bird of prey. In fact the name refers to a man not a beast – specifically the Bailiff of Egle, an official in the Most Venerable Order of St John whose Grand Priory Church stands nearby.

Until 1999 and the reforming of the Statutes of the Order, the splendidly named Bailiff of Egle was one of the Order's five great officers, the others being the Grand Prior, the Lord Prior, the Chancellor and the Hospitaller.

They and their members arrived in London sometime after 1312, when the pope issued a decree abolishing the Order of the Knights Templar and giving their assets to the rival Knights Hospitaller. As it happens, the bulk of their wealth never reached them – Edward II helped himself to a lot of it – but some land close to the City was eventually transferred to the Hospitallers who sensibly appointed the first bailiff to maintain and control their inheritance. It is to be assumed that he was provided with some accommodation during the term of his office, and that this would have stood here in Eagle Court.

EAST PASSAGE, EC1

A narrow alleyway for pedestrians and an ancient right of way, but of little interest to anyone except workers in the Smithfield area seeking refreshment at Ye Old Red Cow fronting on to Long Lane. Run by the well-connected Dick O'Shea in the 1970s and '80s, regulars once included the actors Lord Miles and Sir Peter Ustinov.

ELY COURT, EC1

Hard to find but worth the trouble – the easiest way is to look between Nos 9 and 10 Ely Place – this exceptionally dark and narrow alleyway leads those on foot to the bustling Ye Old Mitre Tavern with its collection of tiny, panelled rooms, one of central London's friendliest and most atmospheric little boozers.

That said, as public houses go it's not especially public. The iron bar down the centre of the opening on to the passage was apparently put there to stop anyone arriving by horse, and even now many of those working locally don't seem entirely sure where it is. As to its origins, however, the name is a bit of a giveaway, the original tavern having been built in 1546 by Bishop Goodrich, Bishop of Ely (see overleaf) as a place for his servants to relax. The tavern wall incorporates a stone mitre from the bishops' old gatehouse although the building itself dates only from 1772. It houses something far older, however, namely the stump of an old cherry tree around which the young Elizabeth I is said to have danced with her future Chancellor.

He was Sir Christopher Hatton, hence nearby Hatton Garden, the Queen in 1581 having (and somewhat outrageously) forced her Lord Bishop to lease a substantial part of his own gardens and a gatehouse to her favourite 'dancing chancellor' at a rent of just £10 a year, ten loads of hay and a solitary red rose.

While popular with his queen, and a skilled political operator, Sir Christopher seems to have been less proficient when it came to personal finance. Debts which were already high in his youth had by 1575 ballooned to an estimated £10,000, and to an astonishing £40,000 when he died in 1591. Perhaps he believed that his debts would die with him but for some reason, with the bulk of that amount owed to the Crown, it fell to the hapless Bishop of Ely to cough up. Already somewhat put upon, he refused, and then died. His successor took a similar stand, at least until a letter arrived addressed to him personally and bearing the signature of his monarch. It read: 'Proud Prelate! I understand you are backward in complying with your agreement: but I would have you know that I, who made you what you are, can unmake you; and if you do not forthwith fulfil your engagement, by God I will immediately unfrock you.' At which point, and left with no choice, the poor fellow is said to have paid up pretty quickly and in full.

ELY PLACE, EC1

Certain of England's loopiest laws seem to have been enacted merely to give trivia book writers something with which to fill their pages, and quiz game compilers something to smile at. You know the kind of thing: how it's illegal to shoot fish in a barrel at Midsummer in a royal park, or how unmarried women in Maidstone may not be seen near the market after dark. Similarly, Ely Place is usually only mentioned in guidebooks in connection with a long-standing (but erroneous) belief that the Metropolitan Police can't enter the street without permission of the Bishop of Ely. In theory that ought to make it something of a thieves' paradise, and on reflection maybe it is, since at least half of the Georgian houses here seem to be occupied by lawyers.

Certainly the story's an enduring one and depends on it having once been the London address of the powerful bishops of Ely who moved here in the late thirteenth century when a row with the Knights Templar meant they had to quit their lodgings in the Temple. Eventually they moved to Dover Street in Mayfair, where they remained until 1909, but the story goes that their ownership of Ely Place meant the little street was technically a part of Cambridgeshire, not London, and was therefore somewhere the Met's writ did not run.

True or not, there's nothing left of Ely House these days, but clearly it was once a very substantial pile, briefly home to John of Gaunt (when revolting peasants wrecked his sumptuous Savoy Palace) and afterwards the venue for an immense five-day banquet. This was for Henry VIII and Catherine of Aragon, the bill of fare for the day including 100 'fat muttons', 51 cows and 24 oxen, 91 pigs, 444 pigeons, 168 swans, 720 chickens, 'capons of Kent nine dozens' and a quite incredible 4,080 larks.

It was also said that the very best strawberries in England were grown in the bishops' abundantly productive gardens, with the local strawberry fayre considered worthy of a mention in Shakespeare's *Richard III*. The place is still worth a visit too, in order to see the little pre-Reformation church of St Etheldreda – London's oldest Catholic church, and possibly England's – which was at one time the chapel and crypt of the medieval Ely House. If nothing else this explains why a relatively small church has such an immense west window, the glass therein depicting the English martyrs of the Tudor period.

FALCON COURT, EC4

Almost certainly taking its name from a long-gone tavern, Falcon Court was once home to the wonderfully named Wynkyn de Worde, sometime apprentice to William Caxton and thus in his own right the second printer in the country.

When he first went into business on his own account he worked from a room in the Swan Tavern, St Bride's Avenue (see p. 157) and then from 1502 until his death in 1534 to a new, larger workshop 'at ye signe of ye Sonne' in 'Flete street'.

As both a printer and businessman, de Worde, an Alsatian expat, was impressively far-seeing. Depending not on wealthy patrons (as Caxton had) but on selling his books to the public, he managed to set, print and produce more than 600 different volumes during his working life and did so despite the laborious nature of those early hand-presses.

He was also the first man to build a book stall in St Paul's Churchyard, soon the centre of London's expanding book trade, and was sophisticated enough to use Italic, Hebrew and even Arabic characters while pioneering printed music.

FAULKNER'S ALLEY, EC1

Its origins lost in antiquity, Faulkner's Alley is known to have been here since at least 1660 and is probably named after a local property owner or builder. This was possibly the man who first developed what would at the time have been a rural spot north of the city – something indicated by a number of nearby streets such as Turnmill Street (or Trimillstrete, for three mills on the River Fleet) and the former Cow Lane, along which animals would have travelled into the capital en route to the market at Smithfield.

FEN COURT, EC3

Here again confusion reigns, with Stow's *Survey* offering a choice of meanings. The first, and perhaps most obvious, depends on the modern meaning of fen, a low-lying area of marshy ground, perhaps as a consequence of 'a long bourne [or stream] of sweet water which of old time breaking out into Fenchurch street, ran down the same street and Lombard Street to the west end of St Mary Woolnoth's church'. But Stow suggests an alternative too, quoting others who are 'of the opinion that it took that name of Fenum, that is, hay sold there, as Grasse [Gracechurch] Street took the name of grass, or herbs, there sold'.

To further confuse matters, perhaps, the area is also sometimes called St Gabriel's Fen, a reference to a neighbouring parish which was amalgamated with St Margaret Pattens when its own church was destroyed in the Great Fire. (St Margaret, incidentally, is Margaret of Antioch, the term 'pattens' being appended to distinguish hers from three similarly named churches in the medieval city, a patten being a kind of crude clog or platform sole sold locally so pedestrians could avoid stepping into the mud and ordure which overlay the streets.)

For a long time, until as recently as the mid-1950s, the court was accessed through an almost tunnel-like archway beneath an ancient building fronting the main street. When that was swept away the sense of seclusion was lost, but more recently a major relandscaping project has rescued Fen Court while providing an engaging connection with the past.

Among others to preach in the nearby St Mary Woolnoth was the Reverend John Newton, author of 'Amazing Grace' and a powerful and charismatic abolitionist who marched alongside William Wilberforce and other leading anti-slavery campaigners. In 2008 Fen Court became home to 'The Gilt of Cain', an intriguing conceptual sculpture created by artist Michael Visocchi and poet Lemn Sissay. The work depicts the podium of a slave auctioneer surrounded by a representation of seventeen sugar canes, the whole piece encompassed by Sissay's words designed to evoke the language of the Stock Exchange trading floor and a number of Old Testament references.

FINCH LANE, EC3

Most often visited, one suspects, for the strangely named Cock & Woolpack pub, Finch is really Fink or Finke, Robert Fink (or Finke), who dismantled and rebuilt at his own expense the church of St Benet in the early sixteenth century. In one form or another this had occupied a site adjacent to this one from the thirteenth to the mid-nineteenth century when, what was by then an Italian baroque design of Wren's, was considered surplus to the requirements of the City's dwindling population and demolished.

With the site given over to the new Royal Exchange, the parish was amalgamated with that of St Peter-le-Poer although this partnership too was to prove short-lived. St Peter's was demolished – when in 1907 the sale of the site raised £96,000 – although the bricks and much of the stonework were reused to build a new church out at Friern Barnet.

FISH STREET HILL, EC3

Originally this led to the foot of an earlier London Bridge and was for a long while called New Fish Street before the crossing was moved upstream. Naturally enough the name referred to the activities of fishmongers – unloading at Queenhithe and later Billingsgate during the reign of Edward I – although today the address is most closely associated with Wren's Monument. Until 1831, at the lower end, the churchyard of St Magnus the Martyr formed part of the roadway to the old London Bridge.

FLEET LANE, EC4

A thirteenth-century byway – possibly older – Fleet Lane would once have run down from Old Bailey to Farringdon Ward Without and to the banks of the eponymous river.

By the late sixteenth century the Fleet was a malodorous and toxic stream of waste and filth and for more than 200 years various attempts were made to improve the river. These were eventually abandoned and what had been a virtual sewer became a de facto one when the whole river was redirected into pipework, arched over and otherwise lost to view.

At that point what had once been a main thoroughfare became a back lane, with a widened Farringdon Street effectively replacing Fleet Lane for anyone wishing to traverse this corner of the City. In 1874 the lane's utility for traffic suffered a further blow, bisected by the lines of the London, Chatham & Dover Railway running into the new Holborn Viaduct station, and Fleet Lane was reduced to little more than a historic cul-de-sac.

Nearby Farringdon Street is worthy of note, however, in particular the site of the Congregational Memorial Hall at No. 8 which was built in 1872 over London's famous old Fleet Prison. It deserves a mention in any political tour of central London, having been the venue of the birth of the Labour Party (at the Trades Union Congress of 1900) and – curiously – of the inaugural meeting of the diametrically opposed British Union of Fascists under Sir Oswald Mosley. Also the administrative headquarters for the 1926 General Strike, the wildly gothic hall was unfortunately demolished in 1969.

FOUNDERS' COURT, EC2

A reference to the Worshipful Company of Founders, a body of independent candlestick and pot makers who in 1389 petitioned the Lord Mayor over complaints about their rivals' shoddy goods.

They received a Royal Charter in 1614 and from 1531 until 1854 occupied a hall on this site, with nearby Lothbury (some say) so named because of the loathsome noises which issued from within. Letting it out piecemeal to other businesses and eventually quitting the court altogether, the Founders relocated to St Swithin's Lane (and more recently to handsome new premises at the corner of Cloth Fair and Bartholomew Passage) but the name has remained unchanged.

FOUNTAIN COURT, EC4

There has been a fountain on this site since 1680, although the present structure is a 1919 recreation of the one by which Charles Dickens arranged for Ruth Pinch to meet John Westlock in *Martin Chuzzlewit*. In 1763 Boswell found it 'a pleasant, academical retreat' and the garden to the south is traditionally held to be the scene of the plucking of the red rose of Lancaster and the white rose of York by Richard Plantagenet and the Earl of Somerset before the civil wars which followed. Here too is Middle Temple Hall, with its double hammer-beam roof one of the finest in Europe; it was the venue chosen by Shakespeare for the debut performance in 1602 of his *Twelfth Night*.

FREDERICK'S PLACE, EC2

A speculative development by the industrious Adam brothers, commemorating a seventeenth-century Lord Mayor, Sir John Frederick, and described by Nikolaus Pevsner as 'an oasis of domesticity' although today it is, naturally enough, all offices.

Bedecked with window boxes when the weather warms up, it is, however, pretty enough and contains a plaque to 'Edwin Waterhouse, Eminent Accountant' – nowhere but London, you might think – and another to the somewhat more eminent Benjamin Disraeli. He worked here in the law but soon left to commence his political career, a lady acquaintance having advised him in 1821, 'you have too much genius for Frederick's Place – it will never do.'

FRENCH ORDINARY COURT, EC3

Burrowing dankly and creepily beneath Fenchurch Street railway station – a survivor of two separate Zeppelin attacks in the First World War – the colourful name refers to an 'ordinary' or eating house, in this case one which in about 1670 was established to serve a local community of French expats. Offering good food at a fixed price, according to Samuel Johnson (who pronounced himself 'tolerably well served'), these Ordinaries were quite common in the City of London, albeit 'not so common here as abroad' – so no change there then.

FRUITERERS' PASSAGE, EC4

Part of the Thames Walk which functions as an underpass beneath Southwark Bridge. It is quite delightful – particularly compared to other sections of the walk such as Steelyard Passage and Queenhithe – and of early 1920s construction.

The name comes from the Worshipful Company of Fruiterers, which traces its origins back to the thirteenth century although the passage was only named as such in 2000, apparently because the company had a warehouse on this stretch of the riverbank.

The passage itself is lined with old tiled murals depicting scenes of old London and attractive scale drawings of the bridge above. The designs for these are based on old drawings and lithographs, the originals of which are held in Guildhall Library, and it seems a great shame something similar cannot be done for grim Steelyard Passage.

FRYING PAN ALLEY, EC2

Back to the Founders in one sense, in that a suspended frying pan or depiction of such on a hanging sign was for a long time a popular way for ironmongers and braziers to advertise their wares on the crowded streets of the medieval city.

These early shop signs of course developed when tradesmen of all sorts, dealing as they were with a largely illiterate public, needed to devise visible, readily identifiable emblems to represent their respective trades.

Some have survived – the bush for a wine-seller, for example, which is of Roman origin and recalls the god Bacchus, with traditionally a bunch of ivy or vine leaves tied to a pole. Others include the pawnbroker's three golden balls, and the blood-and-bandages of the red and white striped barber's pole, which is still popular long after the trade has lost its proto-medical role. Sadly the frying pan has not survived, but perhaps one day soon it could make a welcome return and hang above the door of the traditional greasy spoon café.

GEORGE YARD, EC3

In the sixteenth century there was a wine merchant's shop in one corner of the yard, the publicity-minded proprietor of which tethered a live vulture outside in place of a more conventional shop sign. When his premises fell to the flames on 3 September 1666 he sensibly moved his business to the nearby George Tavern – and the rest as they say is history (see Castle Court, p. 51).

On display here sculptor Charles Wheeler's 1969 'Poseidon Group' was presented to the City by Barclays Bank, and the area should not be confused with George Yard Buildings a mile or so away to the east. Here, in August 1888, Martha Turner or Tabran was found stabbed thirty-nine times in an attack not infrequently cited as one of Jack the Ripper's first.

GLASSHOUSE ALLEY, EC4

Glasshouse Street in the West End recalls the unpleasant trade of extracting saltpetre for glassmaking from domestic effluence. In EC4 there is a similar if less seedy connection, the site between here and Whitefriars Street having been occupied for more than 200 years by the premises of the Whitefriars Glass Company. Manufacturers since about 1680, not just of domestic ware but also of leadlights and stained glass for church windows, the company was acquired in the 1830s by one James Powell, a vintner and entrepreneur, prior to which it may well have been the workshop visited by Pepys in February 1669 where he 'had several things made with great content' although several others were 'so thin that the very breath broke one or two of them'.

Under Powell and his descendants the works prospered throughout the nineteenth century, helped in no small part by the Victorian mania for building and restoring churches. Also a number of well-considered connections with leading names in the Arts & Crafts movement, including Edward Burne-Jones, William De Morgan, Philip Webb and William Morris.

For much of the time the firm's chief designer was Harry James Powell (1853–1922), James Powell's grandson, an Oxford-educated chemist who hearing from John Ruskin that, 'all cut glass is barbarous' concentrated on the other magical characteristics of glass such as 'its ductility when heated and its transparency when cold'.

In 1922, by which time Harry was the head of the firm, the company relocated to Wealdstone in north London, and today its old site is something of a dark place despite the lustrous name.

GLASSHOUSE YARD, EC1

In the seventeenth century the Whitefriars company had at least two dozen rivals in the City alone, one of which was located here, possibly founded by a descendant or associate of the eight Venetian glassmakers who arrived in London as early as 1549. Glass here encompassed every possible kind of application, from mirrors and crown glass through flint glass and window glass to glass for bottles and drinking vessels. Much of it was of such fine quality that in the 1660s John Evelyn was moved to observe that those 'looking glasses' from the works established by the extravagant Duke of Buckingham were 'far larger and better than any that come from Venice'.

GLOUCESTER COURT, EC3

Gloucester Court near Tower Hill was a continuation of Great Tower Street until the turn of the last century when the construction of Byward Street forced a narrowing of the eastern end which was later pedestrianised.

Its most noticeable feature is All Hallows, Barking, founded as a chapel for the abbey at Barking which Eorconweald, Bishop of London, had endowed in 675 for his sister Ethelburga. The church's proximity to the execution blocks of Tower Green and Tower Hill has lent the church some grisly associations: it provided temporary storage for the torsos of John Fisher, the Duke of Monmouth and Archbishop Laud after their respective executioners had discharged their responsibilities.

Judge Jeffreys was married here in 1667 – the church having by some miracle survived the fire. More happily, so too was John

Quincy Adams in 1797, prior to being elected sixth President of the United States of America, and since 1922 it has been the mother church of Toc H, the worldwide fellowship association founded behind the lines of the First World War by a young army chaplain, the Revd Philip Thomas Byard 'Tubby' Clayton CH.

GOUGH SQUARE, EC4

As previously noted, the inestimable Dr Johnson lived in many places – including Johnson Court, though merely by coincidence. He is most closely associated with this little corner of the capital just off Fleet Street and which today is home to the museum which bears his name.

More a compact, L-shaped quad than a square, once hemmed in by elegant Georgian houses – of which, sadly, just one remains – access is via not just the aforementioned Johnson Court but also Hind, Bolt and St Dunstan's. The name comes from its developer, Richard Gough, a wealthy wool merchant whose fame has been all but eclipsed by the square's later, more celebrated occupant.

Johnson himself, of course, was not a local lad but a Lichfield one who after arriving in the capital with his pupil David Garrick took on a fairly peripatetic existence. His biographer Boswell lists no fewer than seventeen different addresses for him, but of these only 17 Gough Square still stands. Outside is a memorial to his 'very fine cat' Hodge, depicted sitting on a copy of the famous Dictionary with an opened oyster.

At a rent of £30 a year Johnson took on the house from 1748 until 1759 (which is to say before he actually met Boswell), its proximity to his printer William Strahan being a deciding factor in his choosing to move here. Today the house is the only Grade I domestic building in the City, having survived not just three wartime raids – scorched beams can still be seen in the attic – but also a lengthy period when its interior was chopped up into cubicles for use by a cheap hotel.

Happily it was eventually rescued by a member of the newspaper-owning Northcliffe–Rothermere dynasty, although its saviour is said to have bought it (for £3,500, in 1910) only because he happened to be strolling by the evening the For Sale boards went up.

It's good that he did, and not just for any architectural merit the place may have had. Johnson may have rented a good many homes in his lifetime but this is *the* one; the one where he lost his beloved wife, and even more significantly (for us, if not for him) the one where he completed his huge enterprise: the first dictionary in English. Johnson had hoped to bring it to the 'verge of publication' within three years; in the end it took him eight, he and six clerks labouring night and day on the top floor of the house to create something whose long, slow gestation even now cannot fail to boggle the mind.

GREAT ST HELEN'S, EC3

Dedicated to the eponymous heroine of Evelyn Waugh's wonderful *Helena*, the mother of the great convert Caesar Flavius Valerius Aurelius Constantinus Augustus, Emperor Constantine the Great. Her church is one of the oldest in the City, with its origins certainly no later than the thirteenth century although there is sadly scant evidence for the claim that it was built by Constantine on the site of an earlier pagan temple.

Unusually it has twin parallel naves, thought to reflect the fact that it was both a parish church and part of a Benedictine nunnery founded by 'William, son of William the Goldsmith'. A screen was erected between the two areas to keep the parishioners and up to ninety nuns separate, but it didn't work and in 1385 the nuns were reprimanded for dressing ostentatiously in showy veils and for kissing their fellow worshippers. Even the prioress was criticised, for keeping too many dogs.

The church is sometimes called the Westminster Abbey of the City, being second only to that one when it comes to the number of memorials and monumental brasses it contains. These include a window recording William Shakespeare's residency in the parish, the tomb of Sir Thomas Gresham (founder of the Royal Exchange and more besides), and a memorial to the wealthy merchant Sir John Crosby who was buried here in 1475.

His home, Crosby Hall, which stood nearby, was clearly substantial, with its own private chapel, guest lodgings, a banqueting hall, debating chamber, a bakery, a brewery, stables and extensive gardens. Today it is the sole survivor of the many such grand City mansions which thronged the City at that time, and as such has been described by English Heritage as 'London's most important surviving secular domestic medieval building'.

That aside, it is also one of the most extraordinary, having gone from luxurious home to City warehouse and back again over the course of 500 years – and moved, brick by brick, tile by tile, from the City to Chelsea Embankment.

At one time owned by Sir Thomas More, Crosby Hall also served as a temporary home for both Sir Walter Raleigh and the future Richard III. At other times it was the head office of the Honourable East India Company, a Presbyterian Meeting House, a restaurant, a commercial store, and for more than a quarter of a century the Crosby Hall Literary and Scientific Institution.

In 1908 the Charter Bank of India bought the site and pulled it down, the building itself being preserved in bits (by the City Corporation and London County Council) and then, nearly twenty years later, rebuilt in Danvers Street, SW3 – coincidentally in the garden of another of Sir Thomas More's houses – for the British Federation of University Women which occupied it for the next sixty years.

In 1988 the by then tired building was acquired by another kind of City merchant, insurance tycoon Christopher Moran, whose enthusiasm for all things Tudor fuelled his desire to restore the hall with its fine double hammer-beam roof, courtyard garden and oriel windows, into a staggeringly beautiful, startlingly ambitious and utterly unique eighty-five-room riverside home.

GREAT ST THOMAS APOSTLE, EC4

A plaque on a low wall opposite Cullum Street records the only church in medieval London to be dedicated to such a well-known saint, but it was not rebuilt after the Great Fire. Instead the parish was amalgamated with St Mary Aldermary, most of the churchyard disappearing as part of a scheme to widen Queen Street. In more turbulent times no fewer than two of the rectors were sent to the Tower, one in 1538 for denying the supremacy of the king and another 120 years later for accusing Cromwell of breaking the first eight commandments (he was interrupted before he got to the final two) and for likening Whitehall to Sodom. A third was sent instead to Leeds Castle, where he died after refusing to take the Oath of Conformity.

GREAT BELL ALLEY, EC2

Once merely Bell Alley – the Old Bell Inn was a seventeenth-century Coleman Street inn – No. 14, another pub, marks the site where in the garret Suffolk-born Robert Bloomfield (1766–1823) wrote the poem that made his reputation. Selling 25,000 copies of 'The Farmer's Boy' even before it was translated into French, Italian and then Latin (*Agricolae Puer*) this enabled him to cease his labours as a cobbler, although in later life he again fell on poor times and died a pauper after failing to make it as a bookseller.

GREAT SWAN ALLEY, EC2

Half the size it once was – the building of Moorgate in 1835 took the rest, as it did with the aforementioned Great Bell Alley – Great Swan Alley once linked Coleman Street with Copthall Avenue and is named after a pub called Ye Swan's Nest which disappeared in 1969. Dominated by the very considerable but prettily decorated neo-baroque bulk of John Belcher's Victorian Chartered Accountants' Hall in Moorgate Place, it is quiet enough today but was the scene of an attempted insurrection in January 1661.

The leader was one Thomas Venner, a cooper and a member of the Fifth Monarchist sect which was active from 1649 to 1661 and took its name from a belief in a prophecy from the Book of Daniel. This supposed that four ancient monarchies – Assyrian, Persian, Macedonian and Roman – would precede the Second Coming. Linking the year 1666 by its numerical relationship to a passage in the Book of Revelation, the Fifth Monarchists expected that year to herald an end to the rule on earth of man. Venner planned to pre-empt this by organising an armed band to seize power for 'King Jesus'. Within less than a week he had been caught, however, and charged with treason. He was quickly hanged, drawn and quartered and the sect more or less fizzled out at that point.

GREEN ARBOUR COURT, EC4

Once part of Turnagain Lane (see p. 199), like several others in the area Green Arbour Court was created by the construction of Holborn Viaduct station in 1874. Even prior to this date, however, there could have been nothing resembling a green arbour in this part of the City and the reference is almost certainly to a tavern of that name.

GREEN DRAGON YARD, E1

There are photographs dating back to 1870 of the Green Dragon, an inn just off Old Montague Street, but despite surviving the loss of the coaching trade – travellers still required stabling for their own horses – both yard and inn eventually fell prey to developers. The origins of the inn itself were almost certainly seventeenth century, but photographs show evidence that parts of the yard had at some time been rebuilt so that the galleries (similar to those which can still be seen at the George, Southwark) were enclosed with elaborate trellised screens or shutters and casement windows.

GREENHILL'S RENTS, EC1

A reference to John Greenhill of Inner Temple, owner of the Castle Tavern in Cowcross Street, who in about 1737 built a series of 'rents' – the Georgian equivalent of our own buy-to-lets – after being refused permission to establish the market he wished to build on the site.

GREYFRIARS PASSAGE, EC1

A reference to a religious foundation established by four Franciscan Friars in Newgate Street in 1224, the passage we see today marks the pathway – always a public right of way – which would have existed between the chancel and nave of the monks' church.

Initially housed by the City's community of Black Friars which had arrived in England some years earlier, the Grey Friars' simple way of life appealed to Londoners and in less than a week the Sheriff, John Travers, offered his house in Cornhill for their use before they moved again on to a parcel of land given by a mercer, John Ewin, by what was then Stinking Lane.

The group of just four soon grew to eighty, their good works among the poor quickly attracting many rich patrons including four queens – Margaret of France, the murderous Isabella of France, Philippa of Hainault and Joan de la Tour of Scotland – two of whom were later buried in the 'cloister garth' together with the heart of Henry II's Queen Eleanor.

As a result of this generous support the monks were able in time to build a massive priory, including a chapter house, dormitories, a library, cloisters and, in 1348, a chapel which at

300ft long and nearly 90ft wide was almost certainly the largest in the country after St Paul's Cathedral.

With the Dissolution all this counted for little, of course, the tombs and memorials being sold as a job lot for just £50 and the church amalgamated with nearby St Nicholas by the Shambles to become Christ Church, Greyfriars. Other buildings were converted to provide accommodation for the new Christ's Hospital, a school for up to 400 poor orphans each of whom was given a blue frock coat and yellow stockings.

Perhaps inevitably the place has a ghost as well, that of Isabella, wife of Edward II and lover of Roger Mortimer. After imprisoning her husband at Berkeley Castle in late 1327 she had him murdered using 'a kind of horn or funnel … thrust into his fundament through which a red-hot spit was run up his bowels'. Today her beautiful but troubled ghost is said to flit through the churchyard garden next door, clutching to her breast the heart of the husband she murdered. The tower, incredibly, is now a private house.

GROCERS' HALL COURT, EC2

Originally a seventeenth-century backwater called Conyhope Lane, after a poulterer's shop sign depicting three rabbits or conies. For a while run-down buildings in the court provided overspill accommodation for the Poultry Compter, a small, locally administered gaol for low-level villains such as vagrants, debtors and anyone convicted of minor misdemeanours such as prostitution or drunkenness.

It was renamed in the twentieth century, the premises of the Worshipful Company of Grocers being at one end of it. This is an impressive, largely 1970s building which replaced an 1893 structure – the company's fourth hall – after this was badly damaged by fire in the mid-1960s. Earlier halls were lent by the company to a variety of other bodies including both Houses of Parliament, Lords and Commons, who moved here briefly following Charles I's attempt to arrest five members of the latter; the Bank of England was here from 1690 to 1734 and a number of Lord Mayors moved in from 1682 onwards.

GROVELAND COURT, EC4

Notable for many years for a pair of massive wrought-iron gates erroneously said to have been presented to the City by William III and Mary II after the royal couple had enjoyed an especially good dinner courtesy of the Lord Mayor. Groveland Court itself is otherwise of little interest but for Williamson's Tavern which – while the present premises are merely pre-war – makes two interesting claims: ownership of the oldest drinks' licence in the Square Mile; and that no pub is further from the boundary walls of the historic City.

GUILDHALL YARD, EC2

Dating back to 1411, although an earlier building with a similar function is known to have existed nearly a thousand years ago, Guildhall is as such by far the oldest and most significant secular building in the City. By the entrance to the yard itself is the old church of St Lawrence Jewry-next-Guildhall, the Lord Mayor's official church, the original of which is thought to have been gifted by the Conqueror himself to the Normandy Convent of St Sauve and St Guingalaen of Montreuil. By the thirteenth century it belonged to Oxford's Balliol College, the master and fellows of which still keep a private pew. The name is derived from the third-century martyr who was either beheaded or roasted on a griddle, and – somewhat paradoxically – the fact that this area was once set aside as a kind of Jewish ghetto before the expulsions of 1290.

GUINNESS COURT, EC1

Devoid of interest and largely residential, like several others in London it is named after the charitable Guinness Trust. This was founded in 1890 by Edward Guinness, great-grandson of the brewer and subsequently the 1st Earl of Iveagh, and for more than 100 years has concerned itself with the plight of the poor of Dublin and London. The present head of the charity is Princess Antonia, the Kaiser's great-granddaughter, who is also the daughter of a Guinness and the wife of the Duke of Wellington's heir.

HALFMOON COURT, EC1

From at least the sixteenth century the Half Moon Tavern stood on the corner of Aldersgate Street, at the time being described in the mid-1860s as 'filled with carved woodwork of the most elaborate kind and the walls are curiously panelled' but sadly closing a few years later. Finding himself locked out one morning, an early customer, one Ben Jonson (1572–1637), repaired to the nearby Sun instead and noted the following:

Since the Half Moon is so unkind to make me go about,
The Sun my money now shall have, The Moon shall
go without.

HARE COURT, EC4

Named after a celebrated MP and Inner Temple Bencher,
Sir Nicholas Hare (1484–1557) of Bruisyard in Suffolk who
courageously defended Cardinal Wolsey in 1530 and was
subsequently appointed Master of the Rolls and Speaker of
the House of Commons. Hare also presided at the trial of Sir
Nicholas Throckmorton who was accused of taking against the
marriage of Queen Mary to Philip of Spain, and after dying in
Chancery Lane was buried in Temple Church. Another, more
infamous judge, Judge Jeffreys (1645–89), also had chambers
here, in the building now occupied by No. 3. Leaving Cambridge
without a degree, he was Common Serjeant of London at the
age of just 26, appointed to the post of Chief Justice of the King's
Bench barely a decade later and was appointed Lord Chancellor
before he was 40. Presiding at what became known as the Bloody
Assizes, he acquired the soubriquet of the 'Hanging Judge', and
is said to have taken great pleasure in watching those he had
sentenced being hanged. Interestingly more than 300 years after
his death from drink and disease, he is still just about the only
High Court judge the average man in the street can name.

HARP ALLEY, EC4

Originally running all the way through to Shoe Lane, Harp Alley was cruelly truncated by the construction in 1868 of St Bride's Street. The seventeenth-century Harp Tavern from which it derived its name has also now gone, formerly opening on to Farringdon Street, while the Guildhall Library has an attractive watercolour by James Findlay (*c.* 1850) showing the National School which once occupied another part of the site.

HARTSHORN ALLEY, EC3

Shortly after meeting Mr Fortnum in St James's, Mr Mason went into business retailing 'hart's horn, gableworm seed, saffron and dirty white candy'. What the latter was for is anyone's guess, but for many years the horns of the male red deer, or rather slender shavings from them, were a source of two useful chemical salts. One was the vaguely medicinal *sal ammoniac* (ammonium chloride) while the other, *sal volatile* (ammonium carbonate), was used chiefly as a smelling salt but also as a detergent for removing stains and as a precursor to baking soda. Hart's horn jelly was also prescribed as a nourishing if somewhat offensive-smelling cure for the runs.

HAT & MITRE COURT, EC1

Curiously named, in that a mitre is a hat, the Hat & Mitre was an eighteenth-century tavern which stood nearby. What at the street end is a very narrow passage opens out at the far end into a small but attractive cobbled garden.

HEN & CHICKEN COURT, EC4

Running off Fleet Street, hard by what many believe to be the site of demon barber Sweeney Todd's infamous shop at No. 186, the name commemorates another long-gone tavern. This one had the rare distinction that Samuel Johnson never dropped in for a drink – at least if Boswell can be believed, since he mentions so many more where, clearly, he did.

HERBAL HILL, EC1

An obvious reference to a herb garden, in this case the one belonging to the London residence of the Bishops of Ely (see Ely Place, p. 84).

HOGARTH COURT, EC3

Originally Fishmonger Alley, Hogarth Court was renamed as recently as 1936 following a suggestion that the celebrated satirist and painter lodged for a while at the adjacent Elephant Tavern. Although long before his fame enabled him to buy his 'little country box by the Thames' – now unfortunately close to the A4, and indeed the Hogarth Roundabout – Hogarth Court is a reminder that he came not from Middlesex but was born in the shadow of St Bartholomew-the-Great where his father Richard was a teacher of Latin and a textbook writer.

HONEY LANE, EC2

In the great tradition of such specialised retail areas as Cornhill and Wood, Bread and Milk Streets, Honey Lane was originally an area known for its bee-keepers and later, for some 500 years of more, for Honey Lane Market. This thrived on a site stretching from Milk Street to Ironmonger Lane, at one time comprising well over 100 stalls, before being cleared away in 1837 to make way for the first City of London School. In 1976 Milk Street was the scene of a remarkable find – a well-preserved piece of mosaic pavement forming part of a high-status Roman building. The quality of the work and its age (AD 90–120) was taken as evidence that by this time London was unequivocally Britain's largest and most important city.

HOOD COURT, EC4

Possibly named after Tom Hood (1834–75) the humourist and playwright son of Thomas, another humourist and poet born a generation earlier above a bookshop in Poultry. The latter was instrumental in the production of *The London Magazine*, while Tom Hood Jr edited *Fun* – a short-lived rival for *Punch* – and launched his own *Tom Hood's Comic Annual*.

HOSIER LANE, EC1

Hidden away in the elbow of Hosier Lane and West Smithfield, Haberdashers' Hall forms the central part of a large 1990s development incorporating shops and apartments as well as office space and the traditional accoutrements of a fifteenth-century livery.

Another of the Great Twelve (and an offshoot of the greatest, the Mercers) the company's royal charter of 1448 united two separate but related divisions, the hatters who made and sold hats and the milliners who imported more fashionable apparel from Italy. The company's first hall was built in 1461 on the corner of Staining Lane and Maiden Lane (now Gresham Street), its replacements being destroyed in the Great Fire and again during the Second World War.

The new hall is emphatically contemporary in its design although it is arranged around a properly secluded, cloistered green quadrangle (not unlike that of a Cambridge College) and displays the kind of superb craftsmanship which is only very rarely seen in modern City exteriors.

The 400,000 bricks used in its sturdy, foot-thick walls, for example, are handmade and held in place by traditional lime mortar. The building also has a traditional, steeply pitched roof, clad using more than 700 handmade, diamond-shaped lead tiles, each of which weighs in excess of 100kg.

Inside too, if one is lucky enough to dine with the Haberdashers, one is assailed by very high-quality workmanship, what the architects call 'a balance between change and tradition', with a vast diagrid timber ceiling, floors of oak and wood panelled walls combining to provide an interior which is at once grand but intimate, strikingly modern yet entirely sympathetic to the old traditions of such a long-standing company.

HUGGIN COURT, EC4

Situated on Huggin Lane, previously Hoggene Lane or Haggen Lane, the name denotes the keeping or more likely slaughtering of swine in this area by the old city dock at Queenhithe.

IDOL LANE, EC3

While over the years plenty of Roman idols have been found beneath the streets and squares of the Square Mile, the name here is thought to be a variation of 'idle'. Suggesting a place to loiter, it thus brings to mind busy Fetter Lane where – despite the air of industry – the name is derived from *fewter*, meaning an idler, from a French portmanteau covering thieves, drunks and prostitutes. Until the 1940s, its most compelling feature was the elegantly pinnacled and buttressed Gothic spire which Wren attached to the medieval St Dunstan-in-the-East. Despite its delicate appearance the church somehow survived the huge hurricane which struck the City in 1703, but was then badly damaged by the Luftwaffe.

INNER TEMPLE LANE, EC4

The highlight of Inner Temple Lane is without doubt the gateway at its northern end, a unique survivor of the Great Fire and as such the City's sole surviving timber-framed Jacobean townhouse. Despite this it was subject to many centuries of abuse, before being rescued and restored barely a hundred years ago.

Originally part of the great twelfth-century estate of the Knights Templar, the stone gateway beneath the Jacobean structure was eventually taken over by the Order of St John of Jerusalem (the Knights Hospitaller) who leased this and much other accommodation in the area to lawyers operating in the area south of Fleet Street. For a while part of the building was a tavern, the Hand Inn, later renamed the Prince's Arms in

honour of James I's short-lived son, Henry (1594–1612), who had recently become Prince of Wales.

Having survived the fire, and been renamed the Fountain, the premises were then leased by a Mrs Salmon to house her popular collection of waxworks. From 1711 until well into the reign of Queen Victoria, Londoners queued to see exhibits including a clockwork waxwork which would kick passers-by, another depicting the execution of Charles I, and the very risqué 'Hermione, a Roman Lady, whose father offended the Emperor, was sentenced to be starved to death, but was preserved by sucking his Daughter's Breast'.

By 1898 the building was decidedly dilapidated, its frontage boarded up, the ancient timbers covered in successive layers of paint, and the then tenant offering passers-by haircuts and steam-powered hair-brushing (seriously). Fortunately, the principal room above the main gateway had survived unharmed, complete with elegant panelling and an elaborate Jacobean plasterwork ceiling which incorporates flowers, three feathers and the initials P.H. for Prince Henry, Prince of Wales.

While there is no documentary evidence to suggest a personal connection with the prince (nor indeed the Victorian barber's claim that it was 'formerly the Palace of Henry VIII and Cardinal Wolsey'), the belief persists that in ancient times it served as the council chamber for the Duchy of Cornwall. Until recently, it was a small museum, housing an exhibition of artefacts on loan from the Pepys Society which could be viewed most weekday afternoons.

IRELAND YARD, EC4

Forever associated with the Bard, the name refers to William Ireland, City haberdasher, who following the expulsion of the Dominican priors of Blackfriars by Henry VIII, came into the possession of some land and buildings here.

In 1612 William Shakespeare moved into the yard, buying a house for £140 – as per a deed of conveyance still held in the Guildhall Library which states, 'now or late being in the tenure or occupancy of one William Ireland … abutting upon a street leading down to Puddle Wharf on the east part, right against the Kinges Majesties Wardrobe.'

While it was well located for Richard Burbage's Blackfriars Playhouse – where the playwright was no stranger, particularly after the Globe in Southwark burned down – Shakespeare was rarely in the house and soon leased it to a man called Robinson before leaving it in his will to his daughter Susanna. An adjacent property was owned by the painter Sir Anthony Van Dyck.

IRONMONGER PASSAGE, EC1

Like nearby Lizard Street and Helmet Row – referencing the company's coat of arms with its distinctive headgear and salamander supporters – the narrow passageway takes its name from a thirteenth-century fraternity which by 1455 had become 'The Honurable Crafte and felasship of the ffranchised men of the Iremonger of the Citie of London'. To the south is another street with a similar connection: Mitchell Street named after liveryman Thomas Mitchell who in 1527 left his estate for the benefit of the Company and its charities.

JERUSALEM PASSAGE, EC1

The St John of Jerusalem was a tavern, pulled down in 1758 to make way for a new parish school and named after the Knights Hospitaller's Priory Church of St John of Jerusalem which had been consecrated by Heraclius, Patriarch of Jerusalem, in 1185.

Built on land given them by a knight, Jordan de Briset, hence nearby Briset Street, the priory brothers took seriously their vows of chastity, obedience and poverty, but by 1381 their order was nevertheless enormously rich. Nor did it help that their prior, as treasurer, was responsible for the hated poll tax and in the Peasants' Revolt that year the priory was attacked and the prior dragged off to Tower Hill for what many considered was a long overdue beheading. The order recovered, however, and the priory was repaired.

Unfortunately, having survived the Dissolution, the bulk of it was later blown up on the orders of Protector Somerset so that the building materials could be carted away to the Strand where he was building a new Somerset House. Only the church survived, and the splendid gatehouse – returned to the Order of St John in 1874 – which now contains its museum and library.

JOHNSON'S COURT, EC4

Dr Johnson lived here for almost ten years, but the name preceded him by centuries, coming instead from Thomas Johnson, 'Cittizen & Marchantaylor of London', who owned property here during the reign of Elizabeth I and died a rich man. He lies buried in the church of St Dunstan-in-the-West, having previously willed his fellow Merchant Taylors the 'some of ffortie and ffive poundes in money to make them a Dynner'.

KING JOHN COURT, EC2

When – and indeed why – St John Court should have become King John's is unclear, but it was built in the sixteenth century on part of the site of Holywell Nunnery, a Benedictine order also known as the Fraternity of St John the Baptist.

The holy well in question has long since disappeared beneath untidy urban development but it is well documented. John Stow found it 'much decayed and spoiled, with filthiness purposely laid there' but it received a longer and more enlightening mention in John Noorthouck's *New History of London* (1773):

> … The third called Haliwell, had its name from a vicinal fountain, which, for the salubrity of its water, had the epithet Holy conferred on it. In King John's Court, Holywell-lane, are to be found the ruins of the priory of St John Baptist, of Benedictine nuns, founded by Robert the son of Gelranni, prependary of Haliwell, and confirmed by charter of Richard I in the year 1189. It was rebuilt in the reign of Henry VII by Sir Thomas Lovell, knight of the garter; who was there buried: and the following ditty was in consequence painted in most of the windows.
>
> 'All the nuns of Holywell,
> Pray for the soul of Thomas Lovell.'

Measured against many other London foundations the nunnery attached to it was never anything but a very small establishment although enclosing much of the ground between Holywell Lane and Bateman's Row gave the nuns space for both produce and seclusion. Nor is there much to see now, although as recently as 2005 concerns were voiced about new development in the area and its impact on what a Museum of London survey team called extensive, well-preserved remains from the medieval priory together with 'medieval garden soils and pitting' and some post-medieval buildings dating from Dissolution to the late eighteenth century on the same site.

KING'S ARMS YARD, EC2

Rebuilt after the Great Fire, the old King's Head Tavern in Coleman Street – by accident or design, it's not known which – was then renamed the King's Arms. At the time the associated Yard ran all the way through to Tokenhouse Yard (see p. 194) but like others in the area it was severely truncated in the 1840s when growing congestion forced a radical rethink of traffic flows and led to large-scale clearances and the construction of Moorgate.

KING'S BENCH WALK, EC4

Aside from Nos 9–11 which were rebuilt in strange, contrasting yellow brick in the early 1800s by Sir Robert Smirke (see Crown Office Row, p. 72), much of King's Bench Walk is of red brick with stone dressings and from outside still looks much as Wren intended it in 1677.

The politician, diarist and philandering biographer Sir Harold Nicolson lived at No. 4 from 1930 to 1945, being ordered out by the Temple Treasurer in July of that year 'as they cannot afford, owing to the loss of premises during the war, to retain residential chambers for non-practising barristers. This is such a terrible blow.'

At the top end is the venerable and wonderfully named Alienation Office, an official body charged with regulating the 'alienation' or unauthorised transfer of feudal lands without a licence from the government. Above the door is the date 1577, although the first regulatory structure to oversee such procedures was established during the reign of Henry III. Subsequent reforms to land conveyancing in the nineteenth century deprived the office of its function and it was abolished in 1835. Today the building houses barristers' chambers.

LAMB'S PASSAGE, EC1

Formerly called Great Swordbearer's Alley – and would that it still was – the passage was renamed in the early 1800s after a property holder in the area called Thomas Lamb. Lamb's buildings still exist, and Mr Lamb also pops up in the annals of the Old Bailey where he appeared as a witness in the case of Thomas Fowler, an apprentice who was indicted for stealing twelve pieces of buckram valued at £5 and selling them to a tailor.

Buckram is a form of stiffened linen or cotton used to bind books, and its manufacture was Thomas Lamb's business. In court he admitted that he had 'been robbed for a great while past' – but clearly a £5 loss was too much to ignore, particularly as Lamb was the apprentice's own master.

Even given such losses, however – the buckram quickly resurfaced in Moorfields, and Fowler admitted his guilt while on remand at Bridewell – Lamb's investments in property meant he must have been a highly successful operator and buckram manufacture a relatively profitable trade.

LAURENCE POUNTNEY HILL, EC4

At one point called Green Lettuce Lane (or Grene Lattyce, meaning an alehouse where wooden lattice covers proved more durable than glass for the windows) and no longer domestic, together with the cobbled Laurence Pountney Lane the present name commemorates the medieval church of St Laurence which stood nearby.

This was built at the expense of a wealthy draper who lived nearby, Sir John de Pulteney. Elected Lord Mayor on no fewer than four occasions in the 1330s, he acquired an old mansion called Coldharbour slightly to the east of where Cannon Street station now stands. This he later leased to the Lord High Constable of England, Humphrey de Bohun, Earl of Hereford and Essex, charging him a quit rent (see Seething Lane, p. 180) of a single rose at midsummer for what was clearly a large and prestigious address.

With their elaborate wooden doorcases Nos 1 and 2 would clearly also have been high-status homes, dating from 1703 after which time new regulations came into force making such obviously flammable and purely decorative features harder to get away with.

To the neighbouring church of St Laurence, Sir John added a chapel and a college with a master and seven chaplains. He, however, chose to be buried in the old St Paul's Cathedral when he died in 1349, possibly of plague, and after being destroyed in the Great Fire his own church – one of many public benefactions he made – was never rebuilt.

LEO YARD, EC1

Once the cobbled yard of the Red Lion Inn, now gone.

LEOPARDS COURT, EC1

Possibly a corruption of Leigh's piece, the present dwellings having been built on the site of a development bought in 1689 by a landlord called Leigh whose descendants retained the property until the early twentieth century. The seller was one Richard Baldwyn, Elizabeth I's Keeper of Gardens and Treasurer of the Middle Temple, both men being commemorated nearby in Leigh Place and Baldwin's Gardens respectively.

LIME STREET PASSAGE, EC3

In the shadow of Lloyds of London, Limstrate or Lime Street first appears in the twelfth century, an area of the City known for the kilns producing quicklime for sale. A potentially hazardous oxide of calcium, quicklime was nevertheless crucially important in the manufacture of glass, mortar and plaster. Caustic and dangerously reactive in water, the same material could be used as a weapon, the eighteenth-century philosopher and historian David Hume recounting in his history of the English how Henry II's navy destroyed an incoming French fleet:

> [Philip] D'Albiney employed a stratagem against them, which
> is said to have contributed to the victory: Having gained the

wind of the French, he came down upon them with violence; and throwing in their faces a great quantity of quicklime, which he purposely carried on board, he so blinded them, that they were disabled from defending themselves.

LITTLE BRITAIN, EC1

Robert Le Breton was a thirteenth-century landowner with several properties around St Botolph's Church, and today the thoroughfare named after him comprises a somewhat confusing cluster of narrow streets and alleys.

The adjacent park at one end has long been popular with office workers looking for a little lunchtime sunshine. Called Postman's Park because of its proximity to the old General Post Office behind St Paul's Cathedral, it is also where in 1900 the celebrated Victorian artist G.F. Watts (1817–1904) proposed siting a national memorial to the selfless heroism of fifty-three ordinary men and women and, more remarkably, young children. Their memorials feature colourful, hand-painted ceramic tiles by William De Morgan, at this time the world's leading practitioner of the art, and include such otherwise unsung heroes as Alice Ayres, a labourer's daughter whose intrepid conduct 'at the cost of her own young life' saved three children from a burning house in Union Street, Borough. Also John Cranmer, a council clerk who 'drowned whilst saving the life of a stranger and a foreigner', and 11-year-old Soloman Galaman who died 'saving his little brother from being run over in Commercial Street'. Worse still, not all were successful: Herbert Maconaghu, a schoolboy, 'his parents absent in India, lost his life vainly trying to rescue his two school

fellows who were drowned'. To the north is the gatehouse of St Bartholomew-the-Great, restored by Sir Aston Webb.

LITTLE TRINITY LANE, EC4

On a site in Knightrider Street, tucked away behind the College of Arms, the church of Holy-Trinity-the-Less was so named to distinguish it from the much grander Augustinian Holy Trinity Priory on Aldgate, the first of the religious houses to be dissolved by Henry VIII.

The lesser building was first mentioned in 1258, and in 1555 the rector, John Rogers, became the first English Protestant martyr to suffer under Bloody Mary. In 1598 John Stow found it to be 'very old, and in danger of falling down', further observing that 'it leaneth upon props and stilts'. But fortunately less than a decade later it was completely rebuilt, mostly at the expense of the wealthy liverymen of the Merchant Taylors' and Vintners' Companies, only to perish in the Great Fire after which the now churchless parish was amalgamated with St James Garlickhythe (see Sugar Bakers Court, p. 190).

LOMBARD COURT, EC3

Banking central and, like the names of nearby Lombard Street and Lombard Lane, a reference to the many northern Italian merchants who arrived here in the early thirteenth century selling woollen goods and gold jewellery. Many of them moved swiftly into money-lending and introduced early forms of insurance following the expulsion of England's Jewish community in 1290 and the sequestration of their assets and property.

Highly successful at this, and over an exceptionally long period, like the Jews before them the Lombards soon fell victim to their own success. Frequently criticised for their high rates, families such as the Riccardis of Lucca, the Florentine Frescobaldis, the Bardis and Peruzzis eventually returned home. Their legacy was to be considerable, however, with several Masters of the Mint coming from Asti and Florence while for centuries the symbols we used for pounds, shillings and pence – £.*s.d* – came from *lire, soldi* and *dinari.*

MAGPIE ALLEY, EC4

Named after the Magpie Tavern in Whitefriars Street – extant in 1761, but long since vanished – and as the street name suggests built over the site of the Friary of the Blessed Virgin of Mount Carmel, the occupants of which were more commonly known by the colour of their mantle as the White Friars.

First hermits and then mendicants, the Carmelites were one of the more popular religious communities in the City. By sticking to their vow of poverty the friars managed to avoid coming to harm in the Peasants' Revolt, and their house remained a place of sanctuary even following the Dissolution. Today nothing above ground survives (but see Ashentree Court, p. 24) and Magpie Alley is thought to mark the position of the monastic dorter or dormitory.

MITRE COURT BUILDINGS, EC4

Built as recently as 1830 on the site of Fuller's Rents and Ram Alley, which used to run into Fleet Street. The name derives from a long-vanished tavern, the Old Mitre, and above the archway into King's Bench Walk is the name of Sir Alexander Croke, a sometime tenant of Fuller's Rents, a Judge of the Admiralty Court and a noted colonial administrator.

MUMFORD COURT, EC2

First recorded as Munford's Court in 1677, presumably after a local landlord or developer, by 1720 the name had changed to the slightly more distinguished Mountford's but has now made something of a return to its original. Either way it has little to recommend it now, being too broad to be mysterious and sufficiently developed – despite the discovery as recently as 2000 of archaeological features dating from after the Roman period, through the Saxo-Norman one and into the early medieval – to have lost what little historical associations it might once have had.

MYDDLETON PASSAGE, EC1

As at Myddleton Square and Myddleton Street, a reference to Hugh, later Sir Hugh, Myddleton, royal jeweller and wealthy seventeenth-century entrepreneur whose brainwave the New River was and who dreamed of transporting unlimited supplies of clean, fresh water nearly 40 miles from Great Amwell and Chadwell in Hertfordshire to a spot near Sadler's Wells.

He did it too, despite the fiercest possible opposition from both those landowners across whose estates his channel would pass and a variety of other vested interests. Myddleton nevertheless committed himself to completing the job in just four years, something which proved a struggle until James I put his shoulder to the task in exchange for half the profits.

Four years later the water began to flow along an open channel 10ft wide and 4ft deep into the Round Pond by Sadler's Wells. Soon Myddleton's New River Company had excavated three more reservoirs, from which sweet water was piped into the City along wooden pipes no leakier than our own, and Myddleton had collected a baronetcy for his efforts. Further reward came in 1862 when John Thomas was commissioned to sculpt him in marble, the resulting figure being presented by the wealthy contract Sir Samuel Morton Peto, unveiled by Gladstone and erected on Islington Green.

NANTES PASSAGE, E1

A clear reference to the Edict of Nantes, the infamous revocation of which in 1685 denied many important civil rights to French Protestants prompting thousands to flee the country. Many ended up in London, working as weavers in and around Spitalfields, while others crossed the river to settle in Wandsworth in what was then still Surrey.

By the early 1700s the number of weavers in Spitalfields may have been as high as 30,000 – Flemish workers as well as French Huguenots, with the latter building no fewer than nine French churches in the neighbourhood, the most famous of which (in Brick Lane) subsequently became a synagogue, a Methodist chapel and then a mosque as the demographic profile of the local population evolved.

Many were hugely successful, with a score or more leaving £5,000 at their deaths, equivalent to more than a million at current prices, and today their legacy is not hard to discern. Besides other Frenchified street names – such as Fournier and Princelet – the most elegant houses in the area, once the homes of successful silk merchants and some exceptionally skilled master weavers, still display the characteristically large attic windows required to admit the maximum hours of daylight for those working away inside.

NELSON PASSAGE, EC1

To look at today it's not much of a memorial to our greatest sea captain, but then besides the eponymous column there is a Nelson Square in Southwark and a Nelson Place in Islington. Elsewhere Nile Terrace and Trafalgar Avenue mark two of the man's key victories, just as Duncan, Camperdown and Napier Streets commemorate other naval heroes.

NEW COURT, EC4

A rare surviving fragment of a Nicholas Barbon original, Middle Temple's New Court was built by the speculator in 1676 on part of the gardens of Essex House in what would then have been the *Outer* Temple. Inherited by Queen Elizabeth's favourite, Robert Devereux, from his uncle the Earl of Leicester, it was the scene of his arrest before he was carried off to Lambeth Palace and then the Tower where he was executed for high treason.

Barbon bought the old house in 1674 and hurried to pull most of it down on hearing that Charles II rather fancied it as a gift for a loyal servant. Within two years he had completed his development, the seven-bay block on the west side that we see today being still very much as he built it, and sold it on to the members of Middle Temple.

NEWCASTLE CLOSE, EC4

Before the construction of the immense, £2.5 million Holborn Viaduct in 1869, what had hitherto been Newcastle Street used to turn sharply to the left to link up with Old Seacoal Lane.

The latter name came from a type of cheap but low-grade fuel. Inferior to charcoal, it was filthy stuff and as early as 1377 Thomas and Alice Yonge informed their lawyer that, besides spoiling the wine and ale in their cellar, 'the stench of the smoke from [a neighbour's] seacoal ... penetrates their hall and chambers so that whereas formerly they could let the premises for 10 marks a year they are now worth only 40 shillings.'

Traditionally called seacoal because it arrived in the capital by boat, much of that shipped to London came from Tyneside – coals to Newcastle and all that – hence the name here, as it is close to where the fuel would have been unloaded on to wharves situated along the River Fleet at a time when barges could travel as far as Ludgate.

NEWCASTLE COURT, EC4

Situated off atmospheric little College Hill where the unexpected highlight is the fine seventeenth-century stone gatehouse to the old Mercers' School. With its memories of the old Whittington College, it gives a view on to the private but charming little courtyard behind as the wooden gates are left open during business hours.

Before the college was built this was Royal Street, a reference not to the Crown but to the area's ancient drink-related heritage (we're in Vintry Ward, from the *Vintarii* or wine importers) and more specifically a thirteenth-century community of French-speaking wine merchants who lived hereabouts. They came from La Réole, a commune in the Gironde department of Aquitaine, which also explains the name of the adjacent church, St Michael Paternoster Royal.

Long after Richard Whittington and his college had gone – the buildings were sold for £92 when Henry VIII suppressed it – property in the area was acquired and developed by a favourite of Charles II, George Villiers, 2nd Duke of Buckingham. In about 1730 his residence was demolished and replaced by a row of smaller houses. Collectively known as Castle's New Court, the name gradually morphed into its current anagrammatic form.

NEWMAN'S COURT, EC3

Formerly Newman's Yard after a seventeenth-century property owner who had a spat with the Worshipful Company of Merchant Taylors over a right of way. The Merchant Taylors are still round the corner in Threadneedle Street and won the dispute, but for some reason Newman's name was allowed to stand.

A hundred years later the yard would have been known to customers of the adjacent Virginia and Maryland coffee house, a popular gathering place for local shippers and merchants which in 1744 changed its name to the Virginia and Baltick to reflect the shifting business interests of its clientele.

By 1810 the thriving coffee house business had moved to the more spacious Antwerp Tavern behind the Royal Exchange. Here, within a few years, the regular customers had formed a committee of senior members, taken over a private room where entry could be restricted and controlled, and devised a set of rules and procedures to prevent the 'wild gambling' which was beginning to impinge on their business dealings.

While the creation of the modern Baltic Exchange was still several decades away, this was the start of the Baltic market as we know it.

NORTHUMBERLAND ALLEY, EC3

Before joining the generalised westward migration of the moneyed, and long before moving into the magnificent ducal palace which for nearly 300 years stood at the western end of the Strand, the Earls of Northumberland kept a large house on Seething Lane.

John Stow recorded a visit in 1598, by which time the family had moved on and the place had become a low gaming house 'common to all comers for their money, there to bowle and hazard'. Soon afterwards it slipped down another rung, becoming a tenement for the very poor.

Remains of the house were discovered during the excavation of the foundations of Friary Court in 1981 – taking its name from the nearby Crutched or Crossed Friars – but this was nothing compared to an earlier find, an authentic Roman pavement, which, after being lifted in 1787 in a pioneering example of rescue archaeology, passed into the care of Burlington House, Piccadilly, and the Society of Antiquaries of London. As previously noted, the society had at this point only recently ceased gathering at the Mitre Tavern in Fleet Street.

NUN COURT, EC2

First recorded in 1720, the name is thought to derive from a local householder or developer rather than having any specific religious connection. As with others in this vicinity, what remains today is merely a portion of the original as a consequence of the driving through of Moorgate in the 1840s to improve access to London Bridge.

OLD CHANGE COURT, EC4

An early attempt at market manipulation, the Old or King's Exchange was established by Henry II in the shadow of St Paul's as a central point where items of value – gold and silver – could be exchanged for currency. It was, says Strype in his survey, somewhere 'for the receipt of Bullion, to be coined. For Henry II. in the 6th Year of his Reign, wrote … that He and his Council had given prohibition, that none, Englishmen, or other, should make change of Plate, or other Mass of Silver, but only in his Exchange at London.'

Andrew Bokerell 'Maior of London' was charged with 'farming' the Exchange, items thus collected being despatched to the Mint while the officers under Bokerell were responsible for the issuance of the dies used for casting the coins and for disposing of these securely when they became worn out. Its precise location is today marked by a plaque in St Paul's Gardens, an area later settled by Armenian merchants and those selling silk and woollen goods.

OLD MITRE COURT, EC4

Another tavern and another literary reference, but here it is Samuel Johnson and James Boswell with the latter discovering that the former's 'place of frequent resort was the Mitre Tavern in Fleet Street, where he used to sit up late, and I begged that I might be allowed to pass an evening with him there soon, which he promised I should'. The two met, enjoyed 'a good supper, and port wine', repairing there again a couple of weeks later after a less than successful evening at Boswell's lodgings in Downing Street.

Other customers included Hogarth and, perhaps somewhat more surprisingly, the Royal Society and the Society of Antiquaries of London, both of whose fellows held anniversary and other formal dinners in the tavern in the mid-eighteenth century.

When its popularity declined (the Royal Society eventually decamped to the Crown and Anchor) it became for a while an auction room. In 1829 it was acquired and demolished by the partners of C. Hoare & Co. in order that their architect, Charles Parker, could extend the premises of this most unique and illustrious bank into and over its ancient cellars which are now the only parts to survive.

OLIVER'S YARD, EC2

First recorded in 1761, but only later renamed after one Thomas Oliver, stonemason, who lived and worked here.

OWEN'S COURT, EC1

Dame Alice Owen *née* Wilkes is recalled now in the name of a co-educational school in Hertfordshire which continues to benefit from an act of charity nearly four centuries old. Alice narrowly escaped being shot in Islington Fields – either by bending down to buckle her shoe or to milk a cow, depending on the teller of the tale. It wasn't quite Cupid's Arrow, but she married the archer Judge Thomas Owen nevertheless, outliving him and two other wealthy spouses, the one a brewer and the last a mercer.

As an old lady, in 1613, she sought to fulfil a vow made that day in Islington and so established almshouses and a school for thirty poor boys of Islington. These, together with her properties, she left to the care of the Worshipful Company of Brewers whose liverymen continue to manage her estate and to use the profits to support the school and education locally.

The school relocated to leafy Hertfordshire in the 1970s but a proportion of the places are still set aside for poorer London children. Alumni include the Hollywood actress Jessica Tandy – born in Geldeston Road, Hackney – and the film director Alan Parker.

OXFORD COURT, EC4

The great mansion of Oxford Place belonged to John de Vere, 15th Earl of Oxford (1482–1540), Anne Boleyn's crown-bearer, and was occupied by the 16th and 17th earls until the last-named disposed of it in about 1580.

Described by Stow as 'one fair and large built house', it had originally belonged to a rich draper, Henry Fitz-Ailwyn de Londonestone, who in 1189 became the first ever Lord Mayor of London. Unlike today's men, who can stand for just a year, Fitz-Ailwyn retained the post until 1213, during which time he did much to improve building and other standards within the walls of the medieval City and secured the future of London Bridge.

Even then he only lost the job because he died, after which his property came into the possession of the brothers of Tortington Priory in Sussex by way of one Robert Aguillum. Unfortunately this left it prey to the depredations of Henry VIII from 1533 onwards, and when the priory was suppressed, many of the possessions – including the London property – were granted to de Vere. Thereafter, it was perhaps not surprising that he renamed it. Nevertheless it is regrettable that the connection with Fitz-Ailwyn was lost and a shame, given his unique status as the first Lord Mayor and his considerable contribution to the life of the City, that 800 and some years later his name is yet to be commemorated on the street map of the capital.

PAGEANTMASTER COURT, EC4

A splendidly evocative name dating all the way back to, er, the early 1990s when the decision was taken to rename an existing address after the official – frequently these days an architect or similar – who is appointed each year by the alderman chosen by his peers to be the following year's Lord Mayor. The pageantmaster's principal responsibility is the Lord Mayor's Show, the first holder having been Richard Baker of the Painter-Stainers' Company in 1566.

Before this renaming the area had been called Ludgate Court, one of the very few alleyways to survive the efficiently clean sweep of this area which accompanied the construction of nearby Ludgate Hill station. This was part of the old London, Chatham & Dover Railway which (despite considerable long-term financial troubles) thrived from 1859 until the 1923 formation of the Southern Railway. For much of that time workmen in the area enjoyed a concessionary flat rate of 1s.

The station itself was located on the Ludgate Viaduct just north of modern Blackfriars station but closed in 1929. It nearly reopened to rejoin the Tube network in the 1970s when plans for the new Fleet Line included a Ludgate Hill Underground station. Instead the proposed route for this line was altered along with the name: Jubilee.

PANYER ALLEY, EC4

Already old by the time John Stow visited in the late 1500s, the name is derived from the activities of local craftsmen making baskets or panniers. For more than 200 years, until 1892, a stone plaque set in the wall of an adjacent house in Panyer Alley Steps confirmed this, reputedly marking the highest point in the City. Together with a little couplet – 'When ye have sought the city round, / Yet still this is the highest ground' – the plaque depicts the figure of a naked youth seated on a pannier and has now been reset in a modern block. The records of the Worshipful Company of Brewers also show a tap or tavern called the Panyer in nearby Paternoster Row in 1430, although modern surveying techniques have since indicated that the City's highest point – by about a foot – is actually elsewhere, in Cornhill.

PASSING ALLEY, EC1

Narrow, dark now the old gas lamp has gone, and with not much to see as you walk through it, it's not just the tell-tale odour which suggests the name has been upgraded in recent years or just slightly misspelled. Either way, the chief joy of Passing Alley is its entrance and exit: an ornate plaster and stonework arch at one end, good honest yellow London stock bricks at the other, but nothing much in between besides a nicely sharp piece of graffito ('aspiration is the best contraception').

PEAR TREE COURT, EC1

The site of an early (1883) development by the Peabody Trust, one of the pioneers of the movement to improve living conditions for the respectable working classes. Pear Tree Court is thought to take its name from an orchard which occupied the site in earlier years, perhaps as part of Clerkenwell's twelfth-century St Mary's Nunnery. This stood to the south and, like the Knights Hospitaller's aforementioned Priory Church of St John of Jerusalem, was founded and funded by a wealthy Norman, Jordan de Briset.

The trust itself was established in the 1860s by George Peabody, an American banker and diplomat resident in London. He was an associate of such reformers as Lord Shaftesbury, William Cobbett and Charles Dickens, the last-named of which may well have had Pear Tree Court in mind when he wrote the description of the 'narrow court' through which Oliver Twist and the Artful Dodger emerged into Clerkenwell Green.

While Dickens wrote and campaigned, Peabody's philanthropy was considerable and wide-ranging, benefiting the education system in the USA as well as building homes here. His initial gift was of half a million pounds, a figure which Queen Victoria described as 'wholly without parallel'. In London the advanced, if occasionally severe, designs which characterised early Peabody buildings were among the very first to include both laundry facilities and play areas for children and even now upwards of 50,000 Londoners benefit from his generosity and vision.

PETER'S HILL, EC4

The church of St Peter, Paul's Wharf, described by John Stow as small – and indeed for centuries known as 'St Peter-the-Little' – existed as long ago as 1170. It was described in 1708 in Richard Newcourt's *Repertorium Ecclesiasticum Parochiale Londinense* as having been 'hung with Turkey carpet for the accommodation of the nobility' during the Commonwealth. John Evelyn recorded a visit here in 1649, but it was not rebuilt after the Great Fire and in 1962 when the churchyard was finally built over, the headstones and memorials were removed to St Ann, Blackfriars. The wharf itself also disappeared long ago, having been given in perpetuity to the Dean of St Paul's by Gilbert de Bruen in 1354 and now only the name exists in this forgotten corner.

PLAYHOUSE YARD, EC4

Supposedly beyond the writ of the City authorities, at the time vehemently anti-theatre, the Blackfriars Playhouse was built in about 1596 by Richard Burbage (1568–1619) within the shell of the old Dominican monastery. The place was popular, the Queen spoke in its favour, but complaints from neighbours meant that he was soon forced to surrender the lease to the choristers of the Chapel Royal. By the time he resumed possession of it in 1608 he was in partnership with his fellow actor, William Shakespeare, whose King's Players performed here.

PLOUGH COURT, EC3

Alexander or Pope Court might be a more appropriate name, the eighteenth-century English poet, satirist and translator having been born there to Edith, wife of Alexander Snr, a linen merchant of Plough Court, Lombard Street. In 1870 the building in which he is thought to have been born was painted by J.L. Stewart and the watercolour now resides in the Guildhall Library Print Room together with two striking black and white photographs documenting the destruction which rained down on the court during the 1940 Blitz. As a result of the latter, not much of interest remains.

PLOUGH YARD, EC2

The yard of the seventeenth-century Plough Tavern, thought to have been pulled down in about 1800. Until it too was demolished in 2007, the yard ran beneath the old North London Railway viaduct. The viaduct was built in 1865, comprised twelve shallow, segmentally arched vaults and ran south to the terminus at Broad Street station which closed in 1986 owing to lack of use.

PLUMTREE COURT, EC4

As with Herbal Hill (p. 110) the likelihood is that the original court was built during the seventeenth century on the site of another orchard forming part of the extensive gardens and demesne of Ely Place. Since being rebuilt it is now dominated by the monolithic premises of accountants and bankers.

POPE'S HEAD ALLEY, EC3

Not unlike the running gag in *Hotel Sahara* (1951) where wartime proprietor Peter Ustinov is forced to replace a portrait on the wall every time his establishment in no-man's-land is occupied by British, Italian, French and German forces – and the odd Arab – the tavern which stood here from the fifteenth until the eighteenth century switched names several times. From the Pope's Head to the Bishop's Head and then back again, the changes were made according to whom was on the throne at the time, and the prevailing mood across England when it came to dealing with the Holy Father and his parishioners.

By contemporary accounts, and regardless of its name, the tavern in question was a substantial establishment, listed as early as 1415 and built on land granted nearly a hundred years earlier to merchants from Florence engaged in the papal service. Strongly built of stone, says Stow, and 'having the Royal Arms on it', the building occupied a large site between Cornhill and Lombard Street.

On 14 November 1666, the place having recently reopened after the Great Fire, Pepys and his wife enjoyed an 'exceeding pretty supper [and] excellent discourse of all sorts' with friends. This was by no means the diarist's first visit and among more than a dozen entries in his hand we find he had previously noted his enjoyment in 'Lumbarde Streete' of the tavern's venison pasty. Years later, flushed with his success in a lecture given at Salters' Hall, the non-conformist Samuel Chandler (1693–1766) similarly chose the Pope's Head Tavern as the place to pick a fight with 'a Romish priest'.

In 1769 the coffee house established a century earlier by Edward Lloyd in Tower Street relocated here and, as the New Lloyds Coffee House, continued to attract a clientele interested in shipping and marine insurance. Besides hosting occasional sales of vessels 'by candle' the proprietor published a weekly bulletin of vessels docking in London and just as this *Register of Shipping* served as the forerunner of today's *Lloyd's List* his establishment – its rules formalised into a professional body just two years later – rapidly morphed into the behemoth that is the modern Lloyds of London.

POPPIN'S COURT, EC4

Perhaps it is no coincidence that Mary Poppins' brolly sported a parrot-head handle, for the popinjay from which this small court derives its name is an Old English word for a parrot-like bird similar to the German *papegai*.

In the fourteenth century the Augustinian abbots of Cirencester kept a house here, called Le Popyngaye, and with the popinjay forming part of their crest it must have seemed an obvious emblem to borrow when it came to naming the court in 1602. The abbots' house is of course long gone, but the bird lives on and is represented in relief above the entrance.

In Thornbury's *Old and New London* (1878) the story is told of William Van Mildert (1765–1836), the last Prince-Bishop of Durham but at the time of the tale just a poor curate living on the other side of Charterhouse Street in Ely Place. Van Mildert found himself in this vicinity one night amid street boys who began firing a volley of squibs in his direction, a squib being a kind of small explosive charge. Finding all hope of escape barred, and dreading the pickpockets who he knew would take advantage of the situation, he loudly exclaimed, 'Ah! here you are, popping away in Poppin's Court!' Incredibly this dreadful pun so pleased the yobs that they at once cleared a path and let him leave. '*Sic me servavit*, Apollo' was his Horatian comment ever after: 'thus did Apollo rescue me'.

The area was also famed in the eighteenth century for its molly-houses, a category of homosexual brothel, one of whose unfortunate keepers was attacked by a mob in the pillory after the courts found that she had 'procur'd and encourag'd Persons to commit Sodomy'. She was Margaret Clap, a wonderfully appropriate moniker if not quite so good as Clarice La

Claterballock, one of scores of 'evildoers and disturbers of the King's Peace' arrested during a clampdown on unrest and immorality ordered by the City authorities in 1340.

POST OFFICE COURT, EC4

In Prince's Street, EC2, an attractive, iridescent blue Corporation of London plaque records that 'Near this spot the General Letter Office stood in Post House Yard 1653–1666. Here were struck in 1661 the first postmarks in the world.' Following the Great Fire it was removed to the premises of the Black Swan on Bishopsgate, and in 1678 it moved again to this small courtyard off Lombard Street.

The new premises had been built over the garden of Sir Robert Vyner Bt, banker, goldsmith to His Majesty the King, the Lord Mayor of London and not infrequently described as the wealthiest man in all England. In 1661 he produced a new orb and a jewel-studded replica of the Crown of St Edward for the coronation of Charles II. Later he famously presented the City with a statue of the king, mounted and trampling Cromwell under foot. Curiously Cromwell sports a turban (the statue these days lives in Ripon), the donor having saved money by modifying an existing work depicting the Polish King John Sobieski crushing a marauding Turk.

At one point Sir Robert was owed the quite staggering sum of £400,000, such was the scale of his personal loans to the Court and State. In lieu of such an amount ever being repaid he was prevailed upon to accept a lifetime annuity of £25,000 – a huge sum. (At this time, in 1672, a gentleman's coach and pair would have cost something under £100.)

PRIEST'S COURT, EC2

Stone-flagged and still with an old wood surround to its entrance, the court would once have been home to the resident priest of St Vedast-Alias-Foster.

With only one other church in the country dedicated to him (at Tathwell, in Lincolnshire) St Vedast was an obscure sixth-century French bishop from northern Gaul. He helped restore Christianity to the region (after decades of destruction at the hands of barbarians) and having accomplished this set about improving the sight of blind men. Foster meanwhile – as in Foster Lane – is thought to be your typical medieval Londoner's best attempt after a few ales at pronouncing such a tricky foreign moniker as Vedast. First it was Fawster or Fauster and then Foster – hence the 'Alias'.

As for his church, it is a bit like the National Trust's Montacute House in Somerset. Twice stripped of its contents, the house has become something of a repository for furniture and artefacts from all over. So too has St Vedast's after taking in orphans from some of the thirteen former parishes it now serves. The organ, for example, was transferred here from St Bartholomew-by-the-Exchange; the seventeenth-century pulpit came from Allhallows, Bread Street; and the font was originally installed at St Anne and St Agnes, Gresham Street.

PRIMROSE HILL, EC4

There's a more famous one further north, and this one couldn't differ more. Its urban location suggests no floral connection; a more likely origin is a builder or property owner of that name who was active in the area.

PRINTING HOUSE SQUARE, EC4

Now gone but still celebrated, the fame of Printing House Square depends on it having been the home of the Walter family and from where, on New Year's Day 1785, *The Times* newspaper was first launched. Initially called the *Daily Universal Register*, just one copy of the inaugural edition survives in the British Library, having been ordered in advance by the Revd Dr Charles Burney, the celebrated Fanny's father.

Remarkably the Walter family retained a proprietorial interest in the presses for the next 181 years – until the mid-1960s – and the building remained a private dwelling until 1910. As well as being one of the very last in the City this also made it the very last instance of a national newspaper proprietor living 'above the shop'.

Unfortunately, together with the square and its garden, what had been the King's Printing Office until its purchase by John Walter was demolished when *The Times* built new offices over the site in 1962.

PRUDENT PASSAGE, EC2

Off-white-tiled and a bit of a squeeze, what was Sun Alley until 1875 is like a miniature version of the Greenwich Foot Tunnel. Linking King Street and Ironmonger Lane, the name change was perhaps made to avoid confusion with several others, similarly named.

PUMA COURT, E1

Joining Red Lion Street at its western end, Puma Court was known as Red Lion Court when it first started appearing on maps of Spitalfields and the surrounding area in the late seventeenth century. It later formed part of the Wood and Michell estate, developed between 1718 and 1728 by Charles Wood and Simon Michell, both of Lincoln's Inn, after some complicated legal shenanigans.

The reason for the name change is obscure, and the developments have now gone, having in 1860 been replaced on the orders of the Commissioners of Works by the wonderfully named Norton Folgate Almshouses. These were intended to replace some earlier dwellings in Blossom Terrace and comprise a charming ensemble of two blocks in parallel, each accommodating eight residents in two storeys with a common staircase serving each block. The design was produced by Thomas Edward Knightley (1824–1905), an architect of some note who was district surveyor for Hammersmith in West London for more than four decades and built the Queen's Hall for Sir Henry 'Proms' Wood.

Recalled by *The Independent* newspaper as 'a dour man with a wretchedly dull sense of what goes into a colour scheme', he produced here a delightful essay in yellow stock bricks, separating the two storeys with a neat corbelled brick band and a slim stone coping to the pediment-like gable ends of the return elevations. Positioned at right angles to the court and pleasantly cottagey, a variety of round and segmental arches and wooden shutters on the windows (with heart-shaped piercings) are not at all what one would expect to find in this corner of east London.

A plaque records, 'These Almshouses Were Erected In The Year 1860 For The Inhabitants Of The Liberty Of Norton Folgate In Place Of Those Built In 1728 Lately Taken Down For The New Street.' The liberty in question provides a historical link with a former landowner, the Priory and Hospital of St Mary Spital, an establishment the liberty outlived before finally being abolished in 1900.

PUMP COURT, EC4

Where Fountain Court has a fountain, Pump Court has a pump – or rather it did have before this was destroyed in a German raid along with the south side of the long, narrow, paved court. The name dates from 1677 making this one of the oldest parts of the Middle Temple although only a few buildings – on the north and west sides, and excluding the shady cloisters which were rebuilt after Wren – are authentically seventeenth century.

QUEENHITHE, EC4

Queenhithe, an extensive dock shown on many eighteenth-century maps but now, particularly at low tide, a very squalid little inlet, was once an important City wharf. Built by Ethelred II (978–1016), making it the oldest dock in the City, it was also the last to go. In what is still considered a serious loss, the buildings on its two wharves were only demolished in the 1970s by a developer wishing to clear the site for a hotel.

For its first 100 years it was known as Ethelredshythe – renamed after the wife of Henry I – and came to comprise Abbey Wharf and

Smith's Wharf, owned by the Worshipful Company of Fishmongers and the City Corporation respectively. The corporation had owned Smith's since the seventeenth century, losing a unique and exceptionally fine mid-nineteenth-century warehouse in yellow stock and gault brick simply because few at the time recognised the true value of mid-Victorian industrial architecture.

RED LION COURT, EC4

The earliest known record of a Red Lion Tavern here dates back to 1592, the place surviving until well into the twentieth century. Sufficiently well, that is, that journalists on the *Melody Maker* – in those days published round the corner at 161–6 Fleet Street – would frequently drop in to interview musicians over a pint. While other pubs in the area boast that Samuel Johnson dropped in, or Pepys, the Red Lion's customers are said to have included members of the Jimi Hendrix Experience and the Bonzo Dog Doo-Dah Band, Spencer Davis and Steve Winwood, David Bowie, Arthur Brown of the eponymous Crazy World, Ornette Coleman, and Peter Frampton. A few even bigger names reportedly missed out on a pint, however: a young Bob Dylan and a scruffy Mick Jagger being among those who were peremptorily ejected by the publisher's ill-informed doorman before an interview round the corner could even be arranged.

RISING SUN COURT, EC1

A popular stop on many guided walks of haunted London, the Rising Sun is a small and traditional eighteenth-century pub, its brown marble and brick façade now restored but derelict for many years (and while owned by Bart's Hospital briefly made over to offices). According to local tradition the upstairs bar was a popular haunt of resurrection men and body-snatchers drawn to the profit potential of 'burking' for the nearby medical school at St Bartholomew's Hospital.

More recently, ghostly footsteps have been reported pacing back and forth across the upstairs bar after last orders, and in the late 1980s two South American barmaids living here claimed to have been woken on several occasions by a someone or something seated at the end of their beds. A year later the landlady, taking a shower one afternoon, heard the locked bathroom door open and close and felt an ice-cold hand run down her back although she seemed to be alone in the room.

ROLLS PASSAGE, EC4

In 1232 Henry II built a chapel for the *Domus Conversorum* or House of Converts – a place of indoctrination for those of his Jewish subjects who had been coerced into renouncing their faith and so had to be kept away from their own community lest they recant. The house, itself stolen from a Jew, provided a communal home and until 1280 a small allowance – equivalent to about 4p a week, slightly less for females – because Jews converting to Christianity automatically forfeited all their possessions to the Crown.

Following the great expulsion of 1290, it was the only way for the Jews of London to remain in London, and approximately eighty chose to live this way in order to avoid deportation. By 1356 the last of these had died, however, although tiny numbers of new converts – men and women, forty-eight in total – continued to arrive until as late as 1608.

Dwindling numbers meant that by 1378 the office of Keeper of the House of Converts had been amalgamated with that of the Keeper of the Rolls and Records of the Chancery of England, or as we would say today, the Master of the Rolls. By this time the house had become his official residence, and the chapel – now more commonly referred to as simply the Rolls Chapel – became part chapel, part repository.

Rebuilt by Inigo Jones, and demolished only in the face of very strong protests, it remained standing until 1896 at the heart of one of London's legal enclaves where the myriad solicitors' chambers soon came to be surrounded by makers and suppliers of horsehair wigs, strongboxes, legal stationery and books.

Given the connection between the two ancient offices represented here, it is perhaps curious to note that England had to wait until 1873 for its first Jewish Master of the Rolls, Sir George Jessel, son of coal merchant Zadok Aaron Jessel.

Because like previous masters he was responsible for the safekeeping of legal documents, what became the Public Record Office (to the Victorians very much the 'strongbox of Empire') was also on this same site. As such it was home to many priceless artefacts, including the original Domesday Book, the triple-locking Doomsday Chest in which the volumes were kept in the Chapter House at Westminster Abbey, the Magna Carta and other medieval records and early state papers. Also Shakespeare's will and those of Handel and Purcell, a polite letter from George Washington to George III, the less polite confession of Guy Fawkes, and the official coronation oath of Queen Elizabeth II.

Sadly the only physical evidence for that first *Domus Conversorum* now is a single stone arch from the chapel, some stained-glass windows, a small portion of mosaic and some funerary monuments – one of which is conceivably the earliest Renaissance monument in the country. These have been built into the fabric of what is now the Maughan Library of King's College in Chancery Lane so seem likely to survive.

ROSE & CROWN COURT, EC2

Linking with Priest's Court (see p. 149) and pleasantly meandering but with little else of interest these days. That said, the Museum of London has several small but colourfully enamelled thirteenth-century glass beaker fragments which were unearthed here by archaeologists, one bearing the enigmatic part-inscription 'ENIMA'.

ST ALBAN'S COURT, EC2

Though the first English Christian martyr, the third-century St Alban had no specific London connection which perhaps explains why just one church was dedicated to him in the capital – Wren's Perpendicular St Alban Wood Street, although even this is now reduced to a solitary, Grade II-listed tower. The foundation date of the church itself is not known – a connection with the Mercian King Offa's eighth-century chapel is disputed – but excavations in the court have revealed Roman materials and ragstone foundations. These are thought to be associated with the large Cripplegate Fort, nearby Wood

Street having originally been laid out by the Romans as a parade ground.

The little garden at the Oat Lane end is all that remains of the site of St Mary Staining, a church burned in the Great Fire and not rebuilt. It is surrounded now by the inevitable towering office developments although happily the striking glass façade at the back of 100 Wood Street curves dramatically and is steeply raked to maximise the daylight reaching the grass and its solitary tree.

ST BRIDE'S AVENUE, EC4

Despite the grandeur of the name, just a narrow alley which leaves Fleet Street and passes between St Bride's Church and the rear of the site of Wynkyn de Worde's Swan tavern (see Falcon Court, p. 85). This is now occupied by another pub, formerly the Twelve Bells & Golden Bell but now called the Old Bell and said to have been built by Wren for his workers.

Long before becoming the journalists' church – or even more grandly, the Cathedral of Fleet Street – St Bride's had been celebrated for its exceptionally long history and rich associations. In the crypt, for example, are preserved the remains of an important Roman house while the foundations of no fewer than seven different churches have been identified on this one site.

The establishment of the first of these has been attributed to Bridget herself, a sixth-century Irish saint from Kildare, although a more ancient Celtic connection may have existed with Brigit, a goddess of fertility. In 1210 King John held a parliament here, and among those married on the site were the parents of Virginia

Dare (the first colonial to be born in America) in 1587. By Pepys' time the burial vaults here were so popular that he had to pay a bribe to a gravedigger to 'justle together' the bodies in order to make room for one more – that of his brother Tom.

When Wren rebuilt it after the Great Fire it was among his most expensive – costing an astonishingly precise £11,430 5s 11d even before the spire was added. It is the latter, Wren's tallest spire even after being reduced following a lightning strike in 1764, which is most celebrated today, not least because the four-storey confection of diminishing octagons is said to have inspired a Fleet Street pastry cook called Rich to create the prototype of the tiered wedding cake we know so well today.

ST BRIDE'S PASSAGE, EC4

Formerly Blue Ball Yard and then Bells Buildings, what in 1909 was renamed St Bride's Passage was home to John Milton until he quit the plague-hit city for Buckinghamshire. Its position marks the boundary of the precincts of the famous church, with the land to the south belonging to the Bishops of Salisbury whose grounds extended as far as the river (see Salisbury Court, p. 175).

ST CLEMENT'S COURT, EC4

Chained to an anchor and thrown to his death in the Black Sea, Clement was a martyred disciple of St Peter the Apostle who was appointed Bishop of Rome in AD 93. The church which bears his name came nearly a thousand years later, the dedication perhaps recognising a maritime connection between the patron saint of sailors and the proximity of the church to the medieval city's bustling wharves.

Almost certainly the St Clements of 'oranges and lemons' fame – its rival St Clement Danes is rather too far west – a less fragrant association was the 1370 plumbers' revolt. Alarmed at the number of lead-smelters setting up their workshops in the area, and suffering as a consequence from the resulting noxious fumes, the locals objected to their presence in the strongest terms possible until the Lord Mayor, John de Chichester, stepped in and ordered the workmen to construct higher chimneys.

ST DUNSTAN'S ALLEY, EC3

Not to be confused with St Dunstan-in-the-West (see overleaf), the tower and shell sandwiched between the alley and the long cobbled vista that is St Dunstan's Lane are all that's left of St Dunstan-in-the-East. The church was dedicated to a tenth-century Archbishop of Canterbury (and sometime Bishop of London) who following his canonisation in 1029 was reputed to have been the most popular saint in England until he was overtaken by the martyred St Thomas à Becket.

Together the tower and ruined nave make an appealing relic of the Blitz, the shrewd decision having been taken not to rebuild yet another Wren church but instead to seek the advice of the Worshipful Company of Gardeners and lay it out as an award-winning garden. One particularly colourful legend about the place suggests the existence of an underground passage running beneath the ruined nave and linking the cellar of Sweeney Todd's famous barber shop with the one situated beneath his girlfriend's pie shop along the way.

ST DUNSTAN'S COURT, EC4

Named for the 'other' St Dunstan's, St Dunstan-in-the-West, although to further confuse matters this had for a long time been known as St Dunstan Over Against the New Temple. This name reflected the fact that the advowson – the right to nominate a new holder to the living – which had originally been granted to the king by the Abbot and Convent of Westminster was then granted by the Crown to the House of Converts (see Rolls Passage, p. 154).

Its preachers briefly included William Tyndale, who later translated the Bible into English, while the poet John Donne was employed as rector here from 1624 to 1631 although he claimed never to have received a penny. His friend, local ironmonger Izaak Walton, first sold copies of his celebrated *Compleat Angler* from a stall in the churchyard. Pepys knew the place too, and recorded being twice rebuffed – once with a pin – by two maids he outrageously attempted to 'take by the hand and the body' during a sermon.

One of relatively few City churches to escape destruction in the Great Fire, but rebuilt in 1829 when it became unsafe, St Dunstan's grateful parishioners celebrated its survival with a large bracket clock which projected over the street and contained two figures – possibly Gog and Magog – who appeared cuckoo-style, to strike the hours. This was later spirited away by the 3rd Marquess of Hertford for his new villa in Regent's Park – the American ambassador's official residence is now on the same site – but was returned to St Dunstan's by the newspaper magnate Lord Rothermere in 1935.

Beneath the clock today can be seen a statue of Queen Elizabeth I, rescued from the old Ludgate when it was demolished in 1760. Thought to be the only one made during the lifetime of the queen, she keeps company with the legendary King Lud, thought by some to be the source of the name London. Together with his two sons he once graced the east-facing façade of the old gateway with Her Majesty on the western one.

ST HELEN'S PLACE, EC3

Arguably the most planned and elegant cul-de-sac in the Square Mile. Curiously French in style, and also known as Little St Helen's to distinguish it from Great St Helen's along the way, its name is derived from the inadvertently sinister-sounding Black Nuns of St Helen's Bishopsgate. This Benedictine nunnery was formed in the early thirteenth century by the son of a wealthy goldsmith but in 1543 much of the property was sold to the Worshipful Company of Leathersellers after being gifted to a nephew of Thomas Cromwell following the Dissolution. Five centuries later the Leathersellers, whose origins are thought to lie with a community of 'whittawyers' or makers of fine white leather who congregated in the shadow of the city walls in the 1200s, still have their hall here. The present building – the company's sixth, seemingly modelled on the Place des Vosges in Paris – is of the mid-twentieth century, its predecessor having been razed to the ground when an incendiary bomb fell on the building next door. The two bronze sculptures flanking the main doorway are by Mark Coreth and represent the ram and the roebuck which form key elements in the company's coat of arms. The latter is represented on the main gates, beneath an unlikely, almost Eddystone-like belvedere.

St Helen's Place is also where the great Mayer Amschel Rothschild's third son, Nathan Mayer Rothschild, first settled upon arriving in London before removing to New Court, St Swithin's Lane, where the illustrious Jewish banking dynasty still has its UK headquarters.

ST JAMES'S PASSAGE, EC3

Now and forevermore associated with Jack the Ripper – on 30 September 1888 Catherine Eddowes was murdered in a dark corner of nearby Mitre Square – the passage which runs into the square lies on the site of the cloister of the Augustinian Priory of Holy Trinity, Aldgate. Founded in 1108, but bankrupt by 1532, it was converted into a home for Sir Thomas Audley, the Lord Chancellor. By descent it came into the possession of the powerful Dukes of Suffolk, hence the naming of the adjacent Duke's Place running into Bevis Marks.

The arrival of Sir Thomas meant that those parishioners who had worshipped at the priory had to move to St Katherine Cree, an arrangement which pleased no one but which prevailed until 1622, when they successfully petitioned both King James and the Archbishop of Canterbury for a church of their own. Unfortunately, once built, the church rapidly became something of a disorderly house. Known in particular for as many as 40,000 illegal marriages, and described by a visitor as 'very dilapidated and dirty and unworthy of description', it was torn down in 1874 and the parishioners sent back to St Katherine's. The site was sold for £6,100 and redeveloped, and today lies beneath the attractive if noisy St John Cass Foundation Primary School. (The eponymous benefactor, son of a carpenter to the Royal

Ordnance, is shown in effigy outside, a copy of the 1751 original by Roubillac which is housed at Guildhall.)

ST JAMES'S ROW, EC1

Keen to regain some privacy from local residents who joined the incumbents of St Mary's Nunnery to pray (see Pear Tree Court, p. 142), the nuns dedicated a small separate chapel to St James which remained in use until the Dissolution in 1539. This mostly stayed standing after the rest of the nunnery was pulled down, but in the seventeenth century fell into disrepair whereupon, the nave having collapsed, the chancel, choir and tower were presented to the people of Clerkenwell as an ordinary place of worship.

While the church was later demolished, rebuilt and then remodelled (in 1842), today nothing remains of the original nunnery although the original Clerks' Well – which stood beyond its eastern wall, and from which the district takes its name – can be seen through a window to Well Court on Farringdon Road, and even visited by appointment. It is located near the junction with Ray Street, formerly Rag Street as so many ragsellers congregated hereabouts, and prior to that rejoicing under the unexpectedly rural-sounding name Hockley-in-the-Hole from whence came the mother of Jonathan Wild, London's self-styled Thief-taker General.

ST JOHN'S PATH, EC1

A component of the veritable warren of passageways which cluster around the old St John's Gate, this narrow covered pathway is clearly shown on John Rocque's celebrated map of 1746 although, sadly, several adjacent paths – such as Red Lyon Stable Yard and Badger's Row – have since disappeared.

Disappearing off St John's Square, this one emerges through a narrow archway onto Britton Street, formerly Red Lyon Street and before that Gardens Alley. Here the Jerusalem Tavern is not quite as venerable as it appears, the sign *Anno. 1720* on its elegant, bay-windowed façade referring to the building rather than the pub itself. At that time it would have been a merchant's house, and later a clock and watchmaker's; the liquor licence was granted only in 1996.

The slightly bizarre house at No. 44, with its diamond-latticed windows and fake-log lintels, was designed for the broadcaster Janet Street-Porter, while the street itself took its new name from Thomas Britton, 'a seller of small coal' who lived in Jerusalem Passage and died in 1714.

A more worthy choice might have been John Britton (1771–1857). A poor orphan who found work as cellarman hereabouts, and later a lawyer's clerk and writer, Britton fortunately soon found his milieu as an antiquarian and pioneering topographer. In 1805 he published the first part of his mighty, nine-volume *Architectural Antiquities of Great Britain*. This was followed by fourteen volumes collectively known as the *Cathedral Antiquities of England* and, after a lifetime spent championing the cause of endangered national monuments, Britton's efforts were rewarded in 1845 with a civil list pension from Disraeli.

Today the existence of such organisations as English Heritage, the Society for the Protection of Ancient Buildings and even the National Trust owes much to his pioneering work in this area. How fitting then that his memorial in West Norwood Cemetery – a vast, vertical slab of brown millstone grit on a grey granite plinth – is now itself a Grade II-listed monument. Considerably taller than a man, it was designed by the editor and architect George Godwin in the hope that it would prove as permanent as Stonehenge.

ST MICHAEL'S ALLEY, EC3

With its famous Hawksmoor tower (see Bell Inn Yard, p. 32), St Michael Cornhill is better without than within, the interior fitments with the exception of an unusual wrought-iron swordstand and a wooden pelican denoting piety having been dispersed or disposed of during an 1860 restoration by Sir George Gilbert Scott.

Outside in the alley the chief point of interest is the picturesque Jamaica Wine House, built on the site of (and so named after) what is held to be the first ever coffee house in London.

On the exterior wall of red Mansfield stone a plaque records, 'Here stood the first London Coffee house at the sign of the Pasqua Rosee's Head 1652', the aforementioned Rosee being a Ragusian manservant (or possibly a native of Smryna, in modern-day Turkey) who after a dispute with his employer opened a coffee house variously known as the Turk's Head and (after 1869) the Jamaica Wine House.

The area already had historic links with the sugar trade and slave plantations of the West Indies and Turkey – Rosee's master

may have been a trader in goods from the latter – and the coffee house rapidly became known for the best rum in the city, the most accurate source of information about shipping to and from the Indies, and for its coffee.

In about 1700 in his journal *London Spy*, Ned Ward cheerfully lampooned the atmosphere surrounding this wildly fashionable new drink. In a typical coffee house, he said (which by this time were numbered in the hundreds):

> there was a rabble going hither and thither, reminding me of a swarm of rats in a ruinous cheese-store. Some came, others went; some were scribbling, others were talking; some were drinking, some smoking, and some arguing; the whole place stank of tobacco like the cabin of a barge … Had not my friend told me that he had brought me to a coffee-house, I would have regarded the place as the big booth of a cheap-jack.

But while Ward lampooned them, the profitable coffee houses and their proprietors thrived. Originally places where both business and pleasure could be enacted, over time some went one way – both Lloyds and the Stock Exchange famously grew out of the coffee house culture – while others evolved into gentlemen's clubs, such as White's in St James's Street, Westminster.

Today, sadly, none any longer serves a good glass of clary – a punchy compound of brandy, sugar and spices – yet it is hard to conceive of a more convivial place to call one's office, or indeed to imagine a successful career in any field being conducted in such informal surroundings. In their late seventeenth-century heyday, however, there was nowhere better than a coffee house to do business. Or to witness what Tom Brown in his *Comical View of London and Westminster* called 'the country of Trade that has turned leather breeches into gold chains, blue aprons into fur gowns, a kitchen-stuff tub into a gilded chariot, a drayman into a knight, and noblemen's palaces into shops and warehouses'.

ST MILDRED'S COURT, EC2

The daughter of one saint, sister to two more, and a saint herself, the West Mercian St Mildthryth (*c*. 660–*c*. 730) had ancestral connections with the Merovingian rulers of Gaul, and is thought to have spent time at the royal abbey of Chelles, now lost but famed for a gold chalice said to have been made by St Eloi.

Returning to England, her religious instruction completed, she was pursued by a suitor but chose to enter the abbey of Minster-in-Thanet (which had been founded by her mother) and became abbess in 694. While she had no specific connection with London, there were two churches dedicated to her within the city walls – St Mildred Bread Street and St Mildred Poultry – although neither has survived.

The court is named after the second of these, but for years was known as Scalding Alley or Scalding Wike after the scalding houses used by medieval poulterers (who give this part of the City its name) to soften the skin to make the process of plucking birds quicker and easier. The church itself was first recorded in 1175, well over a century after the probable date of Mildryth's canonisation, and in the fifteenth century was rebuilt over a covered stretch of the Walbrook. It was rebuilt again by Wren after the Great Fire although, remarkably, the reconstruction work was not finally completed until the late eighteenth century.

In 1872, the congregation having badly dwindled, the church's site was sold for redevelopment. For a while it looked as though the building might live on when a Lincolnshire squire visiting the area was so shocked at the demolition that he bought the remains hoping to rebuild the church on his estate. The building materials were taken by barge to Louth, but when the landowner was hit hard by the agricultural depression, the ancient stonework was used instead to repair farm buildings and field walls.

Today nothing of the ancient courtyard remains either, although the poultry-sellers are commemorated by a relief on a nearby building showing a boy and goose. A pair of plaques record the birth round the corner of the poet Thomas Hood and that the prison reformer Elizabeth Fry lived here from 1800 to 1809.

ST OLAVE'S COURT, EC2

Showing more loyalty to his adopted city than to his fellow Scandinavians, the Norwegian King Olaf Haroldsson (995–1030) spent several years in England fighting alongside Ethelred the Unready – against Danes in general and Canute in particular. Ultimately unsuccessful in the Battle of London Bridge (1014), he was nevertheless canonised and, long popular in England, soon had three churches in London dedicated to him. Tooley Street in Southwark also shares a connection, 'Tooley' being a popular corruption of his name among native Londoners.

North of the river the first of the three, St Olave Hart Street, still stands, and was likened by John Betjeman to a 'country church in the world of Seething Lane' although Pepys received something of a fright here after catching an early sight of plague victims. Dickens, too, called it 'St Ghastly Grim' on account of the macabre carvings of skulls and bones on the stone gateway to Seething Lane. Despite his earlier alarm Pepys was subsequently buried in the nave; elsewhere are the bodies of a 'Mother Goose' and of Mary Ramsey who after her death in July 1665 was generally assumed to have been the first to bring the plague into London.

St Olave Silver Street, however, was not rebuilt after being burned down in 1666. And the third, after which this court is named, was St Olave Upwell Old Jewry (after an old well which stood in the churchyard). This was rebuilt but then torn down under the Union of City Benefices Act (1860) which sought to bring the number of churches in line with the shrinking population.

The sale of the site realised an impressive £22,400 and happily most of the treasures were transferred to neighbouring parishes. The clock went to Hart Street while the bodies in the churchyard were transferred to a new City of London burial ground at Ilford in Essex. Curiously the tower was left standing, and for a while served as the rectory for St Margaret Lothbury before its seemingly inevitable conversion into offices.

ST PAUL'S ALLEY, EC4

On 29 April 1667 the Common Council of the City passed an order requiring a number of small alleyways and passages to be widened to 9 feet 'for the common benefit of accommodation'. One such was St Paul's Alley, thereby making what today must be one of the shortest thoroughfares in the City almost as broad as it is long.

These days, sadly, both ends are kept locked behind two pairs of immense wrought-iron gates. Nor is there any longer evidence of the old Northern Ale-house Tavern which stood here and to which, in 1681, 'all gentlemen and others' called Adam were invited by the innholder (one William Adam) for 'a weekly meeting, every Monday night, of our namesakes, between the hours of six and eight of the clock in the evening'. The idea of these gatherings, according to a strange advertisement he placed in a periodical called *Domestic Intelligence*, was to revive the name of Adam and celebrate it with an 'antient and annual feast'.

ST PETER'S ALLEY, EC3

The certain history of the Palladian St Peter Upon Cornhill goes back no more than a thousand years although John Stow suggests a foundation date of AD 179 describing how:

> The first archbishop of London, in the reign of Lucius, built the said church by the aid of Ciran, chief butler to king Lucius; and also that Eluanus, the second archbishop, built a library to the same adjoining, and converted many of the Druids, learned men in the Pagan law, to Christianity.

The early date is interesting, however, if only because the original church was built on the northern boundary of London's Roman forum and basilica complex. It also incorporated one of the first grammar schools in the capital, although this was clearly not rebuilt when the church was in 1675.

With its distinctive redbrick tower, Wren's new church was substantially restored in 1872 when the carved wooden rood screen fortunately remained untouched. One of only two to survive in Wren's City churches (the other is now in the aforementioned St Margaret Lothbury) this one is rumoured to have been designed not by Sir Christopher himself but (curiously) by his daughter.

Though no longer used as a regular place of worship, St Peter's also still has the seventeenth-century Bernard 'Father' Smith organ on which Felix Mendelssohn performed at least twice in the 1840s during one of several trips to England.

The raised churchyard has also survived and is now a garden, the tombs within it wryly described in *Our Mutual Friend* as being 'conveniently and healthily elevated above the living'. Easily missed, but worth a detour, the alley itself is best entered through a narrow passageway alongside the premises of Ede & Ravenscroft ('Established 1689') in Gracechurch Street.

ST STEPHEN'S ROW, EC4

Slipped into the narrow gap between St Stephen's Walbrook and Mansion House, stone-flagged St Stephen's Row has at the one end Mansion House Place and at the other what is perhaps the most elegant warning against vandalism anywhere in London: 'Caution, any person found sticking Bills or damaging these Premises will be PROSECUTED', it says, the words deeply carved in copperplate into the rusticated side wall of the Lord Mayor's official residence.

The present church, the third on the site, is one of the jewels of the City although its shaded churchyard is sadly closed to the public. Applauded by Lord Burlington, who knew a thing or two, and the sculptor Canova, the church is where Sir John

Vanbrugh chose to be buried and was further described by Ralph James in his 1734 *Critical Review of Publick Buildings, Statues and Ornaments in London* as being 'famous all over Europe and justly reputed the masterpiece of the celebrated Sir Christopher Wren. Perhaps Italy itself can produce no modern buildings that can vie with this in taste or proportion.' It was restored in the mid-1980s, the cost being borne by the developer Peter Palumbo who installed a new altar – nicknamed 'the camembert' – by the sculptor Henry Moore. The latter contrasts with the soaring interior, its vast painted dome more than 40ft in diameter and supported on Corinthian columns and eight arches being the first classical dome to be built in England at this time. The overall effect is gloriously light and spacious but at its installation the Moore altar caused so much controversy that there were moves to have it taken away. Eventually the Court of Ecclesiastical Cases Reserved – this country's highest ecclesiastical court – was forced to rule that Moore's altar was perfectly acceptable as an altar for a Church of England church.

ST SWITHIN'S LANE, EC3

A ninth-century monk who was made Bishop of Winchester, St Swithin is traditionally associated with heavy precipitation on 15 July. According to tradition it rained on that day because, against his detailed instructions, his body was disinterred from its original spot and reburied in Winchester's enlarged cathedral.

The church dedicated to him, St Swithin London Stone (see Salters' Hall Court, p. 176) was an octagonal-domed and -spired Wren masterpiece, but it was sadly not rebuilt following its destruction in 1940 by enemy action. The winding lane is nevertheless an atmospheric little cut-through from Cannon Street to King William Street, with Baron Rothschild's old counting house still recognisable at one end (by its carved representations of the family's famous five arrows) while beneath a small courtyard on the eastern side the Don restaurant occupies the old Sandeman Port cellars where for nearly 200 years the company's sherries, madeiras and ports were stored in barrels before bottling.

SALISBURY COURT, EC4

This was once the entrance to Salisbury House, the London residence of the Bishops of Salisbury which having been virtually incorporated into the original Bridewell for a while looked likely to become – in preference to Whitehall – the capital's principal royal palace.

At one point it was home to Prince Arthur, the sometimes-forgotten Prince of Wales whose death at 15 left the way clear for his younger brother to succeed to the throne as Henry VIII. Thereafter royal interest in the palace of Bridewell weakened and in 1553 it was made over to the City authorities. That part known as Salisbury House was sold a decade later to Sir Richard Sackville, father of the 1st Earl of Dorset, and subsequently renamed Dorset House.

In 1633 in a house on the east side of the court, Samuel Pepys was born, and in 1822 at No. 4 the first-ever edition of the *Sunday Times* was edited by Henry White. Between times a neighbouring house was taken over by Samuel Richardson (1689–1761), an acquaintance of Samuel Johnson and rival of Henry Fielding's. In his own right he was also the author of three highly successful epistolary novels – *Pamela: Or, Virtue Rewarded* (1740); *Clarissa: Or the History of a Young Lady* (1748); and *The History of Sir Charles Grandison* (1753) – and ran a thriving commercial printing house. Richardson also introduced his friend Johnson to the painter Hogarth, the two meeting at his house in 1753 although the latter at first mistook the former for a lunatic in the street outside.

That said, with the exception of No. 1, none of the original buildings survive, as the area has been more or less continually redeveloped since the Great Fire swept through in 1666.

SALTERS' HALL COURT, EC4

Situated behind the famous London Stone, a curious fragment of Clipsham limestone or oolite and one of its oldest landmarks, Salters' Hall Court was also home to its first Lord Mayor, the twelfth-century Henry Fitz-Ailwyn.

There is little mystery to the name, the Worshipful Company of Salters having been licensed in 1394 and today being number nine in the order of precedence as one of the medieval city's 'Great Twelve' livery companies. In today's world of chemical preservatives and reliable technology, it is easy to underestimate the importance of salt to the medieval city, but it is if anything surprising that the company's royal charter was withheld until 1559 given that the substance in which its members dealt was so crucial to so many other City trades.

The original 'Saltershalle' was built on land (bequeathed to the company in 1454 by the Alderman and Sheriff of London Thomas Beamond), close to the Church of All Hallows in Bread Street where many Salters gathered. Badly damaged by fire in 1533, then again in 1539, and again in 1598, in 1641 it was deemed too small and the company moved to a new building 'at the London Stone'. Like many others this fell in the Great Fire, and was rebuilt in 1810 and then again in 1827 when the company's members once more felt they needed more space.

Unfortunately this one too was destroyed – by a German bomb on 10/11 May 1941 – so the present hall, in Fore Street, dates from only 1976. Its highly contemporary style is based on a concept by Sir Basil Spence, the company in the meantime having been billeted in the West End. Today, with the Salters gone, their court and neighbouring Oxford Court are dominated by the wonderfully metallic and curvaceous bulk of the Walbrook Building, one of the area's more imaginative new developments.

SANDY'S ROW, EC2

An important stop on any tour of the old Jewish East End, the building housing the Sandy's Row Synagogue was constructed in 1766 as L'Eglise de l'Artillerie, a community church built at a cost of £400 for the area's growing numbers of French Huguenot refugees.

In line with the shifting population of the area the church eventually passed into the care of a succession of other denominations including the Universalist Baptists, the Unitarian Baptists, the Scottish Baptists, the Salem Chapel and Parliament Court Chapel. In 1867 it was purchased by the Chebrath Menahem Abelim Chesed Ve'Emeth, a Jewish self-help society for the comfort of mourners. This had been founded by about fifty poor Dutch Jews in 1853 as a mutual aid and burial society, eventually evolving into a synagogue for a large but by no means rich congregation who paid a penny per family per week to fund its purchase and restoration. As the Chief Rabbi opposed the establishment of a new synagogue, it was formally consecrated in 1870 by the leading Sephardic rabbi, Haham Benjamin Artom, from nearby Bevis Marks Synagogue.

Following the destruction of the Great Synagogue of London (at German hands on the very night of the bombing of Salters' Hall), Sandys Row Synagogue became the oldest Ashkenazi synagogue in the capital. More recently, despite the Jewish population of the East End being at a historic low, the synagogue has experienced a revival, and plans have been drawn up to use part of this architecturally and culturally important building for a museum. Tracing the history and heritage of early Jewish settlers in London, exhibits are likely to include the unique hoard of Jewish artefacts, prayer books and documents dating back into the eighteenth century which are currently stored in the basement.

SARACEN'S HEAD YARD, EC3

Shown as being unoccupied in the 1891 census, the yard would have been at the rear of the Saracen's Head Tavern which faced on to Aldgate. First recorded in about 1650, and conveniently located to catch travellers journeying to and from East Anglia, the tavern would have stood just inside the old walls.

SCOTT'S YARD, EC4

Burrowing its way beneath the inland end of Cannon Street station, John Stow identifies this fifteenth-century byway as

Carter Lane, a consequence of the number of 'carts and carmen having stables there'. It so happens the headquarters of the City's 'Fraternyte of Carters' – today's Worshipful Company of Carmen – is still in this locality too, at Painters' Hall in Little Trinity Lane. That said, by 1598 when Stow published his *Survey of London*, the name had already been changed to Chequer Alley after a local tavern of that name.

Sadly much of it was swept away with the construction of the station, together with the historic steelyard (or stilliarde, from the German *stalhof*) which in the Middle Ages had been the principal trading base in London for the merchants of the Hanseatic League. First recorded in 1282, and granted royal *Carta Mercatoria* in 1303, what became a fairly extensive walled compound would within a few years have its own warehouses on the river together with a church, counting and weighing houses, and residential quarters set further back.

Extending their trading activities across much of England was eventually to cause problems, however, particularly when English merchants began to suspect that they were not being accorded similar privileges on the continent. With friction turning to violence, the steelyard was closed in 1469 until 1475 when the Hanseatic League finally purchased the site outright. Several league members sat for Hans Holbein the Younger, but their prosperity relative to their local rivals prompted Elizabeth I to take steps to limit their activities before finally rescinding their privileges in 1598. Although reopened under James I, its influence and power gradually weakened and in the Great Fire its buildings were largely destroyed.

In 1853 the site was sold, and work began on Cannon Street station a decade or so later. At the far end from Scott's Yard another narrow pathway, Steelyard Passage, continues the association while a plaque in neighbouring All Hallows Lane dated 2005 commemorates 600 years of Anglo-German cooperation and sixty years of peace between the two nations.

SEETHING LANE, EC3

Originally Shyvethenstrat from the Old English 'sifetha' meaning siftings of chaff, suggesting an area of the city where corn and other cereals would have been threshed.

Seething Lane is directly connected to one of the many small but colourful pieces of historic ceremonial which take place in the modern City, the so-called Quit Rent Ceremonies in which a 'peppercorn' or nominal rent is seen to be paid on ancient properties. Such ceremonies are thought to have been derived from the rent paid on a *hautpas* or footbridge which once passed over Seething Lane linking two properties in the parish of All Hallows Barking-by-the-Tower.

Both were owned by the celebrated soldier Sir Robert Knollys MP (1547–1626), a descendant of the hero of the Peasants' Revolt. His exploits in putting down Wat Tyler's rebels perhaps explains the purely honorific nature of the rent he and his descendants were charged for his unorthodox crossing: a single, perfect red rose to be delivered to Mansion House each Midsummer morning.

In fact, most of the ceremonies of this sort fell into disuse hundreds of years ago, with only a few being revived as recently as 1924 by the Revd 'Tubby' Clayton of All Hallows Barking-by-the-Tower. Since then this particular one has been perpetuated by the Worshipful Company of Watermen and Lightermen, the rose being accompanied to the Lord Mayor's official residence by a uniformed guard of honour comprising winners of Doggett's Coat and Badge. (This gruelling river race predates the University Boat Race by more than a century, is considerably longer, and has been run annually since 1715.)

Other quit rents in the City include 'two knives' payable every year since 1211 for a piece of wasteland in Shropshire. Strictly speaking one was to be 'good enough to cut a hazel rod', the other so poor a blade that it would 'bend in green cheese', although in practice the pair have been replaced by a hatchet and a billhook. A second is payment for 'a certain tenement called the Forge' in the parish of St Clement Danes for which the Queen's Remembrancer is authorised to receive six ancient horseshoes and sixty-one horseshoe nails – even though all traces of the thirteenth-century forge disappeared long ago somewhere beneath the Australian High Commission in the Strand.

SHAFTS COURT, EC3

The shaft in question we know better as a maypole, the one here having at one time been so much larger than the average that the relevant parish church has for many centuries been known as St Andrew Undershaft because the pole was actually taller than the church itself. (The pole, when not in use, would have been stored in the eaves of neighbouring houses and held in place by large iron hooks.)

Unfortunately, on what has become known as 'Evil May Day', some 300 apprentices in 1517 rioted at the perceived privileges of the many foreign traders thronging the City. After further incitement by a preacher, Dr Beal, the Earls of Suffolk and Surrey called in troops to suppress the rioters, eventually taking hundreds

of prisoners many of whom were hanged, drawn, quartered and gibbeted for treason. May Day festivities ceased forthwith.

Left hanging in the eaves for the next three decades, the maypole was then described as idolatrous by a fiery curate from St Katherine Cree – presumably on the grounds that God's church was described as being under it – and chopped up. It was afterwards burned to ashes in the hearths of those houses above whose front doors it had once hung, so that these days the tallest maypole is far from EC3, with the current record going to Barwick-in-Elmet in Yorkshire's West Riding, at something over 85ft.

The church survives, however, and is where, on 5 April each year in one of the City's many small but charming ceremonies, the new Lord Mayor replaces a quill in the hand of John Stow's marble effigy, the great chronicler of London having been buried here in 1605.

SHERBOURNE LANE, EC4

Modern Sherbourne Lane is something of a narrow canyon, and as such of little interest, running diagonally off King William Street opposite the site of the old City Carlton Club. Extant for barely seventy years, an offshoot of the famous Pall Mall original, the latter nevertheless found occasion to host Winston Churchill during his long wilderness years. It was here, on 26 September 1935, that the erstwhile Minister for War and Chancellor of the Exchequer warned his audience that German rearmament constituted 'the greatest and grimmest fact in the world'. Living 'in times of deep and growing anxiety', he said, British rearmament was our 'obvious duty'. His warning was certainly widely broadcast – in the USA even the *Spokane Daily*

Chronicle gave it a full column on page two – but unfortunately many closer to home failed to take heed.

Back in London the name is by no means as old as the lane itself, having been derived from the Langbourne, a stream running into the Thames, and at various times tweaked to give Sharebourne and Southbourne Lane. It has been suggested that the latter referred to the southerly route taken by the watercourse as it wound down to the Thames, but all three variations could simply be prettified sixteenth-century renderings of Shitteborwelane, suggesting that in earlier times the alleyway running into Abchurch Yard (see p. 13) had a far less savoury outlook.

SHIP TAVERN PASSAGE, EC3

Linking Gracechurch Street with Lime Street, and running parallel to Bull's Head Passage, it is clearly named after a tavern, but is best entered beneath another as it can be reached through an archway running under the Swan, one of the City's smallest pubs. Indeed, the Swan is so small that, pressed up against the bar with its stone-flagged floor and bare-brick walls, customers can order only beer.

At the far end of the passage a plaque records the site of St Dionis Backchurch, a Wren rebuilding dedicated to St Denys, the patron saint of France who was rudely beheaded in Paris in the third century. Built right on the south-east corner of London's Roman forum, and one of the many City churches where Pepys is known to have worshipped, the second half of the name is derived from a benefactor called Bac or Bugge. Small but lofty, Wren's design was sadly considered surplus to requirements by the 1850s when the parish was amalgamated with All Hallows Lombard Street.

A parish benchmark dated 1888 can still be seen on a wall in a short walk south in Philpot Lane. And happily the bells of the old church followed the parishioners to All Hallows, while the plate, pulpit and font went to a new church of St Dionis (in Parsons Green, SW6) built using funds raised from the sale of the site.

SOUTH YARD, EC2

Running off Milton Street (see Milton Court, p. 129), South Yard dates back to at least the sixteenth century and would originally have provided stabling for the residents of Chiswell Street. Today with its arched, colonnaded entranceway of brick, and an inclined, cobbled surface ideal for rolling barrels, it is a short but attractive passageway into the yard of the old Whitbread Brewery although the gateway into the latter is only very rarely open.

SPITAL YARD, E1

Cobbled, but somewhat compromised by newer developments and traffic, Spital Yard draws its name from the late twelfth-century New Hospital of St Mary-without-Bishopsgate, later more commonly known as St Mary Spital (hence Spitalfields).

With modern Bishopsgate more or less following the line of the historic Ermine Street heading north to the Roman cities of *Lindum Colonia* and *Eboracum* (Lincoln and York), the original hospital was founded in 1197 on the site of a large Roman burial ground lying beneath what is now Spital Square.

The principal benefactors were Walter and Rosa Brunus or Brown, their foundation soon becoming one of the largest of its type in the medieval world. 'An hospital of great relief', it was run by Austin canons with the help of lay brothers and sisters and was reportedly 'well furnished, for receipt of the poor'. Within a century standards had begun to slip, however, and by 1303 inmates were frequently left without lamps and the sisters seen to be lacking food, money and clothing.

After a visit by the Archbishop of Canterbury the canons were disciplined for 'frequenting the houses of Alyce la Faleyse and Matilda wife of Thomas' and the establishment soon fell into serious debt. Despite its useful function to the City – by 1538 it had 180 beds – both priory and hospital were dissolved in 1539 at the behest of Henry VIII. The chapel and the bulk of monastic buildings were demolished shortly afterwards – although a sermon in its memory is still preached on the second Wednesday following Easter at St Lawrence Jewry-next-Guildhall – with the outer precincts coming under the jurisdiction of the Tower of London and being used as an artillery ground.

Since the sixteenth century builders in this area have been unearthing funeral urns, oil jugs, coins, a couple of 300-year-old bottles of dry Madeira, and more than 10,600 skeletons which have been disinterred by successive waves of archaeologists working here from the 1920s to the 1990s. Dating from the twelfth to the mid-sixteenth century, the majority of these were recovered from the area around the hospital's charnel house, the remains of which were themselves rediscovered in 1999. One of twenty-five medieval buildings on the site, the remains have been carefully preserved on site by the developers of Bishops

Square so that much of an immense vaulted chamber can be seen beneath the pavement outside No. 1.

Working to salvage as much as they could from the site of this vast development – the cemetery alone covered more than an acre – on 15 March that same year a team from the Museum of London recovered a substantial stone sarcophagus containing the beautifully decorated lead coffin of an individual now known as 'Spitalfields Woman'. Subsequent DNA analysis has indicated that she was probably of Spanish ancestry, a high-status Roman citizen whose death warranted some very considerable expenditure. Buried in about AD 350, the Barnack stone coming from the East Midlands, and the lead from Somerset, she was clothed in silk and gold thread, her body surrounded by glass objects and rare jet jewellery and her head resting on a pillow of bay leaves.

STAR ALLEY, EC3

Almost certainly named after the Star Tavern, although today its chief glory is the carefully preserved (if slightly forlorn) fourteenth-century tower of All Hallows Staining. First recorded in 1127, the name is thought to denote 'stain' or stone to distinguish it from several other churches of St Hallows in the city which at this time would have been of wood.

Unusually the church survived the Great Fire only to collapse five years later, it was said because its foundations were weakened by the sheer number of corpses interred too close to its supporting walls. Rebuilt in 1674, it was later united with St Olave Hart Street whereupon the building was demolished, leaving only the tower. This was sold to the Worshipful

Company of Clothworkers for £12,418, the proceeds being used to build a new church at Bromley-by-Bow and the liverymen being obliged to maintain the churchyard and tower thereafter. Briefly, when St Olave Hart Street was bomb damaged in 1941, All Hallows rose again with a prefabricated church known as St Olave Mark Lane occupying the site until 1958 when the restored St Olave's reopened.

Beneath the churchyard, but rarely opened, is a twelfth-century crypt known as Lambe's Chapel Crypt. Its groined roof is supported by short Norman columns, the stonework of which is adorned with zigzag ornamentation typical of the period. It was moved here from Monkswell Street in 1825 where it had formed part of the celebrated Cripplegate hermitage known as St James in the Wall. This had been acquired in 1548 by William Lambe, to whom Henry VIII had granted the site after the destruction by Thomas Cromwell of Garendon Monastery in Leicestershire. On his death, in 1577, the crypt was left to the Clothworkers of whom he had been master – hence its removal to this strange spot.

STAR YARD, WC2

Close to the wonderfully evocative Chancery Lane premises of Ede & Ravenscroft, 'Purveyors to the British Royal Family' and established in 1689 as London's oldest tailor and academic robemaker, Star Yard is named after the old Starr Tavern. It was once open space to one side of the Bishop of Chichester's official London home (see Bishop's Court, p. 35) before being built over in about 1660.

The traditional bollard at one end is modelled on an old 6lb cannon but most of note in the long thin passageway is a rare decorated cast-iron public urinal. Not in use since 1986 or thereabouts, it is of the Parisian *pissoir* sort which was also common in the streets of nineteenth-century London. Painted at different times green or black, and nicely worked, with its elaborate ornamentation including the royal coat of arms, it is now a Grade II-listed structure though rarely open to visitors.

STATIONERS' HALL COURT, EC4

In 1403 the Lord Mayor and City Aldermen approved the formation of a new fraternity or guild drawing its members from London's booksellers (who sold writing materials as well as copying and selling manuscript books) and its limners who decorated and illustrated the manuscripts. These were later joined by the printers who gradually began to dominate the trade and had done so by 1557 when the Worshipful Company of Stationers finally received its Royal Charter.

Initially based nearer to St Paul's, the company's first purpose-built home was raised in 1606, on the site of what John Stow describes as 'one great house builded of stone and timber, of old time pertaining to John, Duke of Britaine'. Subsequently called 'Burgaveny House, and belongeth to the late Lord of Burgaveny' – actually Lord Abergavenny – this was demolished and rebuilt by the Stationers but then lost in the Great Fire together with many of the company's treasures and vast amounts of printed matter valued at an extraordinary £40,000. (Happily one survivor among the latter was a copy of *Hamlett*, by one William Shakespeare.)

Robert Wapshott was quickly commissioned to build a replacement, this time of stone not wood, much of which still stands behind a façade of Portland Stone added in 1800–01 by the Surveyor to St Paul's Cathedral, Robert Mylne.

The company's charter permitted the liverymen to seize illicit or pirated copies and for several centuries 'Entered at Stationers' Hall' was a legend found in every English-language publication, it having been a legal requirement since 1662 for every work printed in Britain to be registered here. In 1710 the law was amended to require a copy to be lodged with the Stationers ahead of publication, and an amendment in 1842 (which remained in force until the Copyright Act of 1911) enabled authors to defend their ownership of a work once it had been registered in this way.

STONE HOUSE COURT, EC3

Running parallel to Cavendish Court (see p. 54) – and backing on to the recently renamed Stone Horse pub – the name is thought to have been derived from a thirteenth-century stone building belonging to the Augustinian Friars. At the time the choice of building material would have marked it out sufficiently from its mostly wood-framed neighbours for it to have become a semi-official name (Brick Court in the Temple was similarly known as Brick Buildings, having been the first in the legal enclave to be constructed entirely of brick).

SUGAR BAKERS COURT, EC3

A narrow passage leaving Creechurch Lane between Nos 22 and 24, the name is derived from the process of sugar refining rather than baking, although many of those involved in processing imported sugar might also have performed some of the tasks which today one would associate more with a confectioner.

In 1677, having escaped destruction in the Great Fire, the place was called Sugar Baker Yard with the slightly more upmarket name being settled upon as recently as 1912 but still retaining the association with what had once been a filthy and unhygienic industry. Writing in 1876, James Greenwood's descriptions of sugar-baking in *The Wilds of London* give some indication as to the hard work involved. He found:

> … dozens of these baking, or, as they would more properly be called, boiling-houses … enormous in size, usually occupying the whole of a street side, and so high that the massy 'mats' of sugar craned up to the topmost storey … Soon as I put my head in at the door of the bakery, the nature of the manufacture in progress was at once made apparent to my senses. Just as unmeasured indulgence in sugar is nauseating to the palate so was the reek of it palling to one's sense of smell. You could taste its clammy sweetness on the lips just as the salt of the sea may be so discovered while the ocean is yet a mile away.

At this time sugar would have been sold in large, cone-shaped blocks rather than in lump or granulated form. To make these, the raw sugar imported into London was boiled up and poured into moulds before being broken into smaller 'loaves' for domestic consumption. By 1875, when he published his book *East and West London*, the Reverend H. Jones estimated that there were just three manufacturers of loaf sugar still active in London, down from nearly two dozen in 1864.

The Crown and Sugarloaf pub in Bride's Lane commemorates the trade (as indeed does Sugar Loaf Court, which John Strype found 'a pretty handsome Place, with a Free Stone Pavement, well built and inhabited') and was reportedly long a favourite among staff of *Punch* magazine.

SUN COURT, EC3

With little to recommend it beyond an attractive, elaborately decorated entranceway – and an intriguing if ultimately disappointing covered passageway running into it off Cornhill – perhaps the best that can be said for Sun Court is that against the odds it has survived.

Neither attractive nor architecturally particularly interesting, it takes its name from a Sun Tavern although this is now long gone. Apparently successive landlords preferred to serve locals rather than the usual office types, an admirable thing to aim for were it not for the fact that this little corner of the Square Mile must ceased to have had a resident population several decades ago.

Those whose office windows overlook the shady little quadrangle probably quite like its peace and quiet. As a visitor, however, one cannot help but feel that this particular public space would look better with a few drinkers and smokers gathered there, or with half a dozen tables at which to sit and chat over a coffee.

SUN STREET PASSAGE, EC2

Sun Street was one of many thoroughfares wholly or partly erased to make way for Liverpool Street station in the 1870s, and now terminates abruptly at Appold Street on the edge of the vast Broadgate Centre development. Sun Street and its Passage were named after an old Sun Tavern (another victim of the railway age) although unusually what was once a very narrow passage running alongside the rails – only wide enough for pedestrians – has since been extended and is now a fully fledged street.

On the piazza at the southern end, below the Liverpool Street station clock face with its incidental Star of David, is a bronze memorial to the children of the *Kindertransport,* commemorating 10,000 Jewish children rescued from the Nazis. Installed in September 2006 it is the work of the Israeli artist (himself a former *Kindertransport* refugee) Frank Meisler and replaced an earlier bronze by Flor Kent. Called 'Für Das Kind', and since transferred to the Imperial War Museum, this had been unveiled three years earlier by Sir Nicholas Winton, who personally rescued 669 children from German-occupied Czechoslovakia. The location for both works was chosen because many of the children first arrived in London by train to Liverpool Street station.

TALBOT COURT, EC3

A traditionally flag-stoned and cobbled alley – somewhat surprisingly given its entirely contemporary entry point on Gracechurch Street – today Talbot Court is dominated by the Swan pub (dating back to 1825, when it was the Old Ship

Tavern) although its name references an earlier, pre-Fire hostelry commemorating the popular hunting dog or possibly a medieval tabard.

TILNEY COURT, EC1

Originally this was known as Tripe Yard, the immediate vicinity having been a traditional 'shambles' (from the medieval word 'shamel' meaning booth or bench and a 'flesshammel' specifying this as a butcher's stall). Despite the inevitable mess and carnage, John Strype found it 'very small and ordinary' in his 1720 expansion of Stow's work, the *Survey of the Cities of London and Westminster*, and by 1770 or thereabouts much of the property was owned by an Anne Tilney, hence the change of name. Interestingly Strype Street, E1, named after John Strype's father, was known as Tripe Yard until 1903.

TOKENHOUSE YARD, EC2

Built during the reign of Charles I on the site of the house and garden of the 20th Earl of Arundel, Tokenhouse Yard was developed by Sir William Petty and took its name from an office charged with the production and delivery of 'farthing pocketpieces' or tokens which were traditionally issued by many city tradesmen.

With very few exceptions copper coins were not widely circulated in England until 1672 – Elizabeth I was particularly prejudiced against what was called 'black money' – but smaller denominations were sorely needed by the general population of the City and so upwards of 3,000 tradesmen and others at this time issued and accepted tokens for the purpose, often made of lead.

By 1607 it was reported that some £15,000 worth were in circulation in the City and in 1613 King James was urged to issue official farthings in order to stem the flow of what was in effect a private currency. Charles I followed suit, but during the Civil War a shortage of copper meant that tokens again sprang to prominence. Later Charles II had new halfpenny and farthings struck at the Tower using Swedish copper, declaring these to be legal tender in 1672 so that the tokens gradually fell into disuse.

TOOK'S COURT, EC4

Built in about 1650 by Thomas Tooke, a wealthy City landowner, the L-shape of Took's Court conceals an intriguing piece of wartime – and Cold War – infrastructure. In the 1940s, at Churchill's insistence, it was decided to build a series of eight deep-level shelters, each one designed to accommodate 8,000 in safety in twin tunnels 16ft 6in in diameter and around 1,200ft long.

Four of the eight – at Camden, Clapham North and South, and Belsize Park – were equipped with latrines, first aid posts and so on for civilians to use during air raids. The others were secret citadels intended purely for official use, with Stockwell providing emergency accommodation for the US military, another beneath Goodge Street serving as General Eisenhower's European HQ, and the last two beneath Clapham Common and Chancery Lane being set aside for the civil authorities against attack by V2 rockets.

Following the defeat of Hitler, plans were drawn up to link them into a new high-speed north–south 'super tube' but nothing came of this. Instead seven were turned over to storage – the British Library declined one of them – although interestingly the lease agreements allowed for these to be rapidly reoccupied by the authorities should the need arise.

Only Chancery Lane remained in official hands, being first used to store an estimated 400 tons of top-secret documents and then later incorporated into a giant subterranean 'atom-proof' telephone exchange. Located 100ft below Took's Court, with an anonymous entrance on High Holborn, its own accommodation, sickbay and catering sections for 150 staff and supplies for a six-week lockdown, the exchange also contained the famous Cold War 'hotline' linking the Kremlin and the White House.

When relations between the two superpowers thawed sufficiently for the scheme to be abandoned, the vast underground facility was offered for sale for offers around £5 million. Until as recently as 2000, however, it was still possible to see the facility's ventilation shafts in Took's Court (the entrances of the other seven deep-level shelters are also still there to be seen) but subsequently the site has been developed and now nothing remains above ground.

TOWER ROYAL, EC4

The site of medieval lodgings known as the Tower Royal and situated on Cannon Street. Far from being regal, the name is a corruption of Réole, the building having been purchased or leased in the thirteenth century by wine merchants from this region of Bordeaux.

The lodging itself was nevertheless a substantial building, and in 1320 it passed into the possession of Edward II who gave it to Queen Philippa a decade later. She extended the property for use as her wardrobe until her death when it passed to the Dean of Westminster at a rent of £20 a year and then to Joan, Princess of Wales (1328–85). Following the successful suppression of the Peasants' Revolt in 1381 she was visited here by her son, Richard II, who came to give her the good news. According to John Stow he was here again in 1386 when he received the exiled King Leon VI of Armenia, to whom he granted a pension of £1,000.

Eventually the building fell into decline – it was used for stabling horses during the reign of Henry VIII, and later divided into tenements – and following its destruction in the Great Fire it was not rebuilt. Today the name is attached to a plain cul-de-sac with barely room to turn a car.

TRIG LANE, EC4

Formerly Fish and then Sunlight Wharf, and these days little more than a car park abutting the concrete canyon of Lower Thames Street. The wharf at Trig Lane was operational until 1982, however, and reportedly had the last working crane on the Thames, its name coming from the Trigges, a family of fishmongers resident in the area in the fourteenth and fifteenth centuries.

Today there is little of interest beyond the view across to the rebuilt Globe Theatre, although archaeological surveys of this stretch of the shoreline have thrown up a high concentration of natural resin beads as well as bone, coral, stone, glass and wood fragments dating from the eleventh to the fifteenth century – and the remains of an ancient oak wharf.

More remarkable still was the 1974 discovery of a pair of bone-riveted spectacles. They were found in what had been a medieval rubbish dump behind the river wall, and are now in the Museum of London. Thought to date from about 1440 and made from bone from the front leg of a bull, they are similar to spectacles depicted in continental paintings of that period and to a pair uncovered by a Dutch archaeologist at Bergen op Zoom in 2001. Because of this it is thought that they may have been manufactured in London by an expat spectacle maker from the Low Countries.

TRINITY SQUARE, EC3

Laid out in front of the headquarters of Trinity House, more correctly known as The Master, Wardens, and Assistants of the Guild, Fraternity, or Brotherhood of the Most Glorious and Undivided Trinity, and of Saint Clement, in the parish of Deptford Strond.

Still active today this is the body responsible for pilotage, buoys and lighthouses around the coast (as it has been since 1514) the square having at its other extremity another building with maritime associations, namely the looming bulk of the heavily Edwardian Port of London Authority building, and the immense Portland stone Mercantile Marine Memorial by Lutyens.

Designed by Sir Edwin Cooper in 1912, and towering more than 165ft above the square, the PLA's showy and somewhat bombastic headquarters managed somehow to circumvent the 1894 London Building Act which for fire safety and other reasons outlawed anything over 100ft. This was perhaps because the upper half housed nothing more than a vast statue of the god Neptune – in the event of a fire there would therefore have been no one on the building's upper levels in need of rescuing – but perhaps also because at this time the PLA was at the very peak of its powers and perhaps not easily dissuaded from its chosen path.

TURNAGAIN LANE, EC1

As apt a name as possible for a byway which once ran down to the rank River Fleet, whereupon one was forced to walk back the way one had come. Until the river was covered over it was called Wendageyneslane and ran down from Old Bailey, and as Stow put it – there being no bridge – 'it turneth down to Turnemill brook, and from thence back again, for there is no way over'. Then it was a cul-de-sac but today it is barely more than a large triangular lay-by to Farringdon Street.

VINE HILL, EC1

A dead-end for traffic – pedestrians can continue up a run of steps to Roseberry Avenue – L-shaped Vine Hill occupies part of the aforementioned gardens laid out by the Bishops of Ely, subsequently taken over by Sir Christopher Hatton and at some point laid to vines.

WARDROBE PLACE, EC4

In the mid-thirteenth century what we know as St Andrew-by-the-Wardrobe was 'St Andre de Castello', a reference to the nearby Castle Baynard which had belonged to a knight of that name in the Conqueror's retinue. By 1361 its name and that of nearby Wardrobe Terrace had changed, recognising the acquisition by Edward II of the former townhouse of Sir John Beauchamp which stood immediately north of the church.

Edward used the building as somewhere to store his robes and ceremonial dress as well as funerary garb and 'cloaths of state, beds, hangings and other necessaries for the houses of foreign ambassadors, cloaths of state for Lord Lieutenant of Ireland, Prince of Wales and ambassadors abroad'. Household account books were also kept in the building for the royal family, the place being so commodious that the king was prevailed upon to offer the rector of neighbouring St Andrew's 40s annually for the loss of tithes.

For a while the Master of the Wardrobe was Sir Edward Montague, a cousin of Samuel Pepys, but in 1666 the place was razed to the ground and, rather than rebuild, the Royal Household moved its effects to a riverside position close to the Savoy.

At this point the garden of the 'Kinges Majesties Wardrobe' was developed into what Strype describes in 1720 as 'a large and square court, with good houses'. Sadly much of this was demolished in 1982, but Strype would recognise Nos 3–5 which are of that date and the place still has an authentically historic feel once the workers have departed. Indeed, after dark, an apparition of a lady dressed in white or pale grey has been observed moving from one doorway to another although with little sense of urgency or distress. Unfortunately though, in the

way of these things, she disappears if one looks directly at her or attempts to start a conversation.

WATLING COURT, EC4

A connection is inevitably drawn between this and the Roman route from London to St Albans. However, the Watling Street from which one steps into Watling Court was until the 1400s known as Athelyngestrate, meaning the street of a prince or noble. Later simplified to Atheling Street it would become Watheling Street before being tweaked again in the eighteenth century to give us the name by which we know it today.

There is, even so, one small Roman association to the place as one of south-east England's oldest mosaics was found here, believed to date from the late first or early second century. Principally composed of a pinkish material known as *opus signinum* – made from lime, water and crushed tile, and of North African origin – it is decorated with mosaic roundels and little crosslets which are set into it at regular intervals.

WHITE BEAR YARD, EC1

An unappealing cul-de-sac, the name a reference to a tavern named after a polar bear belonging to Henry II. Something of a celebrity in thirteenth-century London, this animal was accommodated in the Tower Menagerie which had been established by King John as early as 1204. Having already received three leopards as a wedding present from the Holy Roman Emperor, Frederick, Henry's collection was augmented by a white bear and an elephant, gifts from the kings of Norway and France in 1251 and 1254. The public was admitted to the menagerie on payment of a small fee, or – it was said – if they brought along an old dog or cat to supplement the bear's diet.

WHITE LION COURT, EC3

Running off the east end of Cornhill opposite St Peter's Church and not to be confused with the hideous White Lion Hill. Clearly the names of both Court and Hill were derived from local taverns, of which today nothing remains although the oldest property in the court, dating from about 1780, has two lions guarding the entrance. Now an insurance office, from 1834 to 1901 the building was used by the publisher of *Lloyd's Register of Shipping*.

WINE OFFICE COURT, EC4

Early on in their friendship Dr Johnson famously advised Boswell, 'Sir, if you wish to have a just notion of the magnitude of this city, you must not be satisfied with seeing its great streets and squares, but must survey its innumerable little lanes and courts.' It is likely he had somewhere just like this in mind, it being 'not in the showy evolutions of buildings, but in the multiplicity of human habitations which are crowded together, that the wonderful immensity of London consists'.

As the name suggests, this narrow passage with its mounted cannon once housed the Excise Office responsible, until 1665, for authorising the licences required for retailing wine in the City. It appears under this name in John Ogilby's map of 1676, the cartographer being a resident of the Court at that time, as indeed was Oliver Goldsmith when he began writing *The Vicar of Wakefield*. Today, however, the place is best known for one of London's most famous taverns, Ye Olde Cheshire Cheese, which as the board outside proudly declares has been trading successfully through the reigns of fifteen monarchs. In truth it is the only interesting thing here.

While it is not true that Dr Johnson compiled his famous dictionary while living off ale and biscuits provided by the pub, as a local he would have known it and it seems likely he would have visited here with friends and associates such as Sir Joshua Reynolds, Edward Gibbon, David Garrick and, of course, Boswell.

The present pub arose from the ashes of the Great Fire in 1667, but the place clearly had a previous life with the cellars incorporating part of the undercroft of the northern gatehouse to a 600-year-old Carmelite monastery. The front step looks a good deal older too, protected as it is by an iron guard but beneath this worn thin by hundreds of years and many thousands of feet.

To writers and journalists it has long been known as 'the House', and indeed one of the first chapels of the National Union of Journalists was formed here in 1907. Nor has its real name anything to do with dairy produce, being instead derived from a sixteenth-century landlord by the name of Thomas Cheshire.

Nearly four centuries on one of his successors behind the bar had a pet parrot who achieved a good deal of publicity when it celebrated the Armistice by fainting after mimicking the sound of 400 champagne corks popping open. Also renowned for a very full (and offensive) vocabulary, the bird died in 1926 at the age of 40 and was honoured with obituaries in more than 200 newspapers around the world. With the death of Fleet Street – the *Sunday Express* was the last to move out, abandoning its gleaming black art deco home in 1989 – the journalists are now long gone, and while they still do food here, nothing on the menu quite equals *Ye Pudding* for which 'the House' was once well known. Accorded a mention in *The Forsyte Saga*, and weighing between 50 and 80lb, this took up to twenty hours to boil and had 'entombed therein beefsteaks, kidneys, oysters, larks, mushrooms and wondrous spices and gravies, the secret of which is known only to the compounder'. On a breezy day, it was said, it could be smelled as far away as the Stock Exchange.

Appendix I

STREET NAMES WITHIN THE SQUARE MILE

If it is true that history is written into the streets of London (and within the Square Mile there is famously none called 'road'), the street names – including those previously described – are very much the index.

ALDERMANBURY, EC2

The site of Saxon 'burgh' or 'bury', an enclosed settlement belonging to an 'earldorman'. This was the high official of a district, charged with raising and collecting taxes, administering the law and raising an army when required to uphold the law. In its modified form the term survives today to describe a member of the City's legislative body.

ALDERSGATE STREET, EC1

Leading out of the City via Ealdred's Gate. Like Moorgate this was a later opening through the City walls and was rebuilt in 1670 but removed less than a century later. Its precise location has been identified as having been opposite 62 Aldersgate Street.

ALDGATE, EC3

One of the oldest of city names, and a reference to one of the original gateways – named Eald, 'old' or possibly 'ale-gate' suggesting the presence of an inn on the road into and out of the city.

APOTHECARY STREET, EC4

A reference to the Worshipful Company of Apothecaries whose hall was built here within a couple of decades of their foundation in 1671.

APPOLD STREET, EC2

John George Appold (1800–65) was a Shoreditch-born fur dyer and engineer. He invented the centrifugal pump, demonstrated an innovative curved vane at the 1851 Great Exhibition at the Crystal Palace, and designed a crucial braking mechanism for laying the first sub-oceanic telegraph cable in 1857.

BARLETT'S COURT, EC4

The King's Printer, Thomas Barlet or Bartlett, was granted property in the area by Edward IV.

BARNARD'S INN, EC1

The townhouse belonging to a fifteenth-century Dean of Lincoln, John Mackworth, which was subsequently occupied by a man named Barnard. His name was retained when the property was leased to a group of Chancery lawyers. It is now the home of Gresham College.

BASINGHALL STREET, EC2

Named after the Basings, a wealthy and influential mercantile family possibly from the Hampshire town of the same name, who had a house here in the thirteenth century. The derivation of Bassishaw High Walk is similar, 'haw' being an Old English word for yard.

BILLITER SQUARE, EC3

A billiter or 'belzeter' was a medieval bell-founder, many of whom would have been employed in the old city which was so abundantly provided for in terms of churches and bell towers.

BISHOPSGATE, EC2

The name, which makes several appearances on this side of the City, almost certainly references St Erkenwald, a seventh-century Bishop of London whose sister – St Ethelburga – has a tiny church dedicated to her in the vicinity. (Rebuilt after a terrorist bombing in 1993, the peaceful little courtyard behind St Ethelburga's was subsequently remodelled on an Andalusian garden with, at its centre, a Bedouin-style tent with Moroccan mosaic floors and Turkish carpets.)

BLOMFIELD STREET, EC2

Formerly Broker Row, but renamed after Charles Blomfield, Bishop of London from 1827 to 1857, who boosted the number of clergy to serve the growing city population and fathered the architect Sir Arthur Blomfield.

BOUVERIE STREET, EC4

An eighteenth-century street named after William Pleydell-Bouverie, Earl of Radnor. Pleydell Street is nearby.

BRACKLEY STREET, EC1

Built on the former gardens of the Earl of Bridgewater's house, one of his subsidiary titles being Viscount Brackley – hence neighbouring Viscount Street, Bridgewater Square, etc.

BREAM'S BUILDINGS, EC4

Although evidence of his true identity is now lost, it is probable that property in this area was built or occupied by a Mr Bream or Breem.

BRICK LANE, E1

Before development began in the seventeenth century the area was dug out for earth to make bricks and tiles, the lane itself just a muddy carters' track bringing building materials into the city.

BROKEN WHARF, EC4

As long ago as 1249 a wharf in the area was described as 'broken' or in a poor state of repair. This was almost certainly due to a long-running dispute about the division of responsibilities between its joint owners, the Abbey of Chertsey and the Abbey of Hamme – which took the best part of half a century to resolve.

BUCKLERSBURY, EC4

The thirteenth-century 'Bokerelesbury', meaning the 'burgh' or settlement of Bukerel or Bucherel family who owned property here in the eleventh century.

BURGON STREET, EC4

No longer new, in 1885 what had hitherto been New Street was renamed after John William Burgon (1813–88) Dean of St Paul's.

BUSH LANE, EC4

Recalling the presence of a Bush Tavern as long ago as the 1400s, a bush at that time being a common sign outside many inns. In an echo of the ancient tradition of hanging vines or green branches outside such establishments, it was a useful way to attract the illiterate imbiber.

BYWARD STREET, EC3

Named after the nearby Byward Tower, which is itself so-called because of its proximity to the Warder's Hall. It is from here the senior warder emerges each evening to secure the Tower of London precincts following the celebrated Ceremony of the Keys.

CAMOMILE COURT, EC3

Named after the camomile or earth-apple plant, *Matricaria recutita*, which in earlier times would have been grown here for its important medicinal properties.

CANNON STREET, EC4

Originally Candelewrithstrete, later Candlewick Street, and so a reference to candle and tallow manufacture rather than makers of artillery pieces.

CHISWELL STREET, EC1

Chiswell is an Old English term meaning a place with poor, stony or gravelly soil – and so ripe for development.

CLOAK LANE, EC1

A name whose derivation is not known, despite its relatively recent coinage. First mentioned in 1677, it was before this date known as Horseshoebridge Street after a crossing on the Fleet.

CLOTHIER STREET, E1

The location in the late nineteenth century of a popular clothes market specialising in used and worn garments.

COUSIN LANE, EC4

William Cosin, Sheriff of London in the early fourteenth century, lived in a house on or near this site.

CREECHURCH BUILDINGS, EC3

A corruption of Christchurch, the buildings occupying part of the grounds of the Priory of the Holy Trinity Christchurch.

CRIPPLEGATE STREET, EC2

A reference to the Crepel Gate in the city walls, meaning a covered gateway rather than one reserved for the disabled. That said the corruption 'cripple' may have been adopted after the body of St Edmund the Martyr passed through the gateway prompting a legend to spring up suggesting that 'cripples' could be cured by sitting or sleeping in the gateway.

CROSSWALL, EC3

A thoroughfare which crossed the line of the old city walls, remains of an old Roman bastion – one of as many as eleven – having been identified beneath here and at America Square (p. 18).

CRUTCHED FRIARS, EC3

Members of the Friary of the Holy Cross in the thirteenth century could be readily identified by the large cross they wore as an emblem and which led to their being known as the Crossed or Crutched Friars. Their establishment stood nearby in Hart Street, and the Cheshire Cheese at No. 48 is surprisingly atmospheric for a pub squeezed beneath a railway.

CULLUM STREET, EC3

Sir John Cullum (1699–1774) was a Suffolk baronet and London landowner who served as a Sheriff of the City of London.

CURSITOR STREET, EC4

Close to the office of the Coursiter, a sixteenth-century official charged with serving Chancery writs.

DISTAF LANE, EC4

A distaff or 'rock' is a cleft stick used to hold the wool or flax used in spinning suppliers of which would have been active in this area in the medieval city.

DORSET RISE, EC4

A reference to Thomas Sackville, Earl of Dorset (see Salisbury Court, p. 175).

EAST HARDING STREET, EC4

In 1513 the Worshipful Company of Goldsmiths was bequeathed a number of properties in the area by Agnes Hardinge. West Harding Street is nearby.

FLEUR-DE-LIS COURT, EC4

With no connection to the Prince of Wales the name is thought to be derived from an old shop sign.

FORE STREET, EC2

Originally Forestrete, a thoroughfare standing in front of the medieval city walls.

FOX AND KNOT STREET, EC1

While not a natural pairing the name is derived from a mid-eighteenth-century tavern of this name which stood nearby.

FRIDAY STREET, EC4

Another reference to fishmongers and to the ancient practice of eating fish on Fridays – widespread in England before the Reformation – when the markets around Cheapside would have been especially busy.

FURNIVAL STREET, EC4

The townhouse of Sir Richard Furnival stood nearby and in the late fourteenth century was leased to a group of lawyers to become Furnival's Inn. This survived the Great Fire but closed in the nineteenth century.

GARDNERS LANE, EC4

A nineteenth-century name, prior to which it had been known as Dunghill Lane – a name for which no further explanation is necessary.

GILTSPUR STREET, EC1

A reference to the area having once been popular among spurriers, makers of spurs who advertised their trade with signs depicting golden or gilded spurs. Notable today is one of London's last remaining watch-houses, built to prevent bodies being stolen from the churchyard by suppliers to nearby Bart's Hospital.

GODLIMAN STREET, EC4

Of unknown origin and a poor substitute for the street's earlier name, St Paul's Chain, from a sixteenth-century barrier erected to prevent traffic crossing the churchyard during services.

GOODMANS YARD, E1

Goodman was a tenant farmer working land here owned by the nuns of St Clare's Convent (see Minories, p. 217).

GOPHIR LANE, EC4

A corruption of a medieval surname, Gofaire, who perhaps owned or leased property in this area.

GREAT WINCHESTER STREET, EC2

Acquiring a parcel of monastic property following the Dissolution, Sir William Powlett, Lord Treasurer, bequeathed it to his son Lord Winchester.

GUTTER LANE, EC2

Originally Guthrun's Lane, probably recalling a Danish property owner.

HARROW PLACE, E1

A representation of a harrow was a popular sign over a metal-worker's shop, any number of whom would have worked in the old city.

HENEAGE LANE, EC3

Following the Dissolution, land formerly owned by the Abbey of Bury St Edmunds (see Bevis Marks, p. 33) was acquired by the courtier Sir Thomas Heneage.

HOLBORN, EC1

A bucolic reference to the infamous Fleet, a bourne (or stream) in a hollow.

HOUNDSDITCH, EC3

Popularly assumed to be a reference to a stream or ditch into which dead dogs were thrown although it is highly unlikely that medieval Londoners preferred this one ditch over many others when it came to matters of canine disposal. More likely is that hounds for hunting were kennelled here, conveniently located for the forests once lying to the north and east of London.

INDIA STREET, EC3

George Street was renamed immediately prior to the First World War, taking the new name from the extensive warehouses nearby of the East and West India Docks Company.

JEWRY STREET, EC3

Originally Poor Jewry or Little Jewry Lane, distinguishing the Jewish settlers here who were markedly less well off than their higher status kinsmen living closer to Guildhall around Old Jewry.

JOHN CARPENTER STREET, EC4

A fifteenth-century town clerk of London and a benefactor whose bequests laid the foundations of what became the City of London School.

KINGHORN STREET, EC1

A curious renaming of King Street, a name which by 1885 was one of so many within the capital that it was felt to be in need of adjustment.

KNIGHTRIDER STREET, EC4

Possibly a reference to an early processional route, with John Stow in 1598 suggesting that knights rode this way to the tournament ground at Smithfield.

LEADENHALL COURT, EC3

In the early 1300s the house of Sir Hugh Neville acquired this name because of its unusual lead roof. Within a century or so this had disappeared to be replaced by the celebrated market of the same name.

LEMAN STREET, E1

In the seventeenth century the family of Sir John Leman, Lord Mayor in 1616, owned land on the very edge of the City. Nearby Mansell, Prescot and Alie Streets all commemorate marriages contracted by the offspring of his family with individuals of these names.

LIVERPOOL STREET, EC2

Named after the Conservative statesman Robert Jenkinson, Lord Liverpool (1770–1828). Originally known as Old Bethlem, after the famous hospital 'for the distracted', the street was widened and improved the year following his death.

LOTHBURY, EC2

A 'burgh' or settlement of Hlothere's people, a name thought to date from the seventh or eighth century.

LOVAT LANE, EC3

A corruption of 'love'.

LOVE LANE, EC2

A street already popular with prostitutes by the time John Stow published his *Survey of London* in 1598. A coaching inn, the Swan with Two Necks, was a popular departure point for travellers heading north.

MINCING LANE, EC3

Land here owned by the Clothworkers' Guild in 1455 was formerly held by a community of minchins, from the Old English *mynecen* meaning nun.

MINORIES, EC3

Established by St Clare of Assisi in about 1215, the Sorores Minores – or Little Sisters – had a church here from the late thirteenth century which became the parish church in 1538 but was demolished in the 1950s.

MUSCOVY STREET, EC3

Commemorates the Muscovy Company, a group of Tudor merchants trading in Russia who received a Royal Charter in 1555 and enjoyed a monopoly on trade with that country until 1698.

NEW LONDON STREET, EC3

A reference to a local property owner rather than to the city in which he lived.

NICHOLAS LANE, EC4

The church of St Nicholas Acons stood nearby, the name a corruption of Haakon and a reference to a Danish benefactor who established the church and dedicated it to his patron saint, a Bishop of Myra who fell foul of the third-century Emperor Diocletian but lives on as Santa Claus.

NORTON FOLGATE, E1

The site of the north tun or town, a parcel of properties belonging to the Folegate family.

PATERNOSTER ROW, EC4

Prior to the Reformation which swept away such things, makers of rosary beads (or paternosters) and other ecclesiastical supplies would have set out their stalls as close as possible to St Paul's Cathedral.

PETTICOAT TOWERS, E1

From the market, still extant, where clothes formed an important proportion of those goods sold.

PHILPOT LANE, EC3

Sir John Philipot (c. 1330–84), who was Lord Mayor of London, occupied a house on this site and married Landy Joanne de Saundeford. He was buried in the rich and fashionable Grey Friars Church.

PLOUGH PLACE, EC4

A reference to an 'ordinary' or eating house of this name which stood here in the sixteenth century.

PORTSOKEN STREET, E1

A 'soke' was a discreet area enjoying certain privileges and freedoms in medieval London, this one being beyond the gate or port of the City and later lending its name to one of the City wards (see Appendix II).

PUDDLE DOCK, EC4

John Stow refers to 'one Puddle that kept a wharf on the west side thereof … many horses watered there'.

RADNOR STREET, EC1

The Earls of Radnor were governors of the French Hospital, built in 1718 for the city's population of Huguenot refugees. When this was closed in 1866 the street was built across part of the grounds.

ROOD LANE, EC3

In the early sixteenth century a large rood or cross was erected in the yard of St Margaret Pattens while the church was being rebuilt. Once this was completed, in 1538, the rood was taken down and destroyed lest it became an object of superstition.

ROPEMAKER STREET, EC2

First recorded in 1672, the name refers to local manufacturers producing rope for general and industrial usage rather than marine.

RUSSIA COURT, EC4

More likely a corruption of rushy, as a topographical description, than a reference to any connection with Russian trade.

ST ALPHAGE HIGH WALK, EC2

Close to the site of a church to the Norman saint and Archbishop of Canterbury.

ST BENET'S PLACE, EC3

St Benedict or Benet of Nursia was a fifth-century religious reformer, the founder of Western Christian monasticism who published his *Rule* for coenobitic monks (that is those who live within communities). Comprising seventy-three short chapters, the *Rule* laid down instructions about living a spiritual life on earth and how to run a monastery efficiently.

ST CLARE STREET, EC3

See the Minories, p. 217.

ST MARTIN'S-LE-GRAND, EC1

The name refers to the size and status of the medieval church of this name which stood here until 1538.

ST MARY AXE, EC3

Built not later than 1200, and closed in 1560, the church contained an axe said to be one of three used by Attila the Hun to behead an English princess and her 11,000 virgin handmaidens while on a pilgrimage along the Rhine.

SAVAGE GARDENS, EC3

In 1626 a house here was occupied by the wealthy Thomas, Viscount Savage of Melford Hall, Suffolk. His widow Elizabeth died penniless after backing the wrong side during the Civil War.

SERJEANTS' INN, EC4

Until 1873 High Court Judges were also Serjeants-at-Law and from the early 1500s until 1730 the Serjeants' Inn was accommodated in a mansion formerly owned by the Archbishops of York.

SERMON LANE, EC4

No connection with Amen Corner or Creed Lane but more likely a corruption of Sarmoner's Lane after Adam le Sarmoner, a thirteenth-century landlord.

SISE LANE, EC4

From St Sythe or St Osyth, more familiarly known as 'Toosey', the seventh-century martyr.

SMOKEHOUSE YARD, EC1

Self-explanatory, particularly as the smokehouse – complete with strange pivoting, iron window shutters – still dominates the small square.

SNOW HILL COURT, EC1

With its tiny private gardens concealed behind St Sepulchre-without-Newgate, the original name – Snowrehille or Snore Hill – derives from an old word for twist, Snow Hill at one point having followed an even more sinuous course than it does today.

SUFFOLK LANE, EC4

Recalls the Manor of Roses, a property owned by the Dukes of Suffolk and in the mid-sixteenth century given to the Merchant Taylors' Company for use as a school.

SWEDELAND COURT, E1

Suggestive of a small Scandinavian community, one of three in and around the City including one close to the site of the Mansion House which had its own Lutheran church.

TALLIS STREET, EC4

After Thomas Tallis (*c.* 1505–85) composer, organist and Gentleman of the Chapel Royal, and suitably close to the original premises of the Guildhall School of Music.

TELEGRAPH STREET, EC2

Formerly Bell Alley but renamed following the establishment here of the Telegraph Office of the General Post Office in the 1870s.

THREADNEEDLE STREET, EC2

Originally Three Needle Street, almost certainly after a medieval shop sign, although by happy chance the Hall of the Worshipful Company of Merchant Taylors is still to be found at No. 30.

THROGMORTON AVENUE, EC2

After Sir Nicholas Throckmorton or Throgmorton (*c.* 1515–71), an English diplomat and politician, ambassador to France, and heavily involved in the fraught relations between Elizabeth I and Mary Queen of Scots.

UNDERSHAFT, EC3

A reference to a traditional 'shaft' or maypole, a generally harmless diversion which was banned in the City following the May Day rioting of 1571 (see Shafts Court, p. 181).

VINE HILL, EC1

Built over the gardens and vineyard of the London residence of the Bishops of Ely (see Ely Place, p. 84).

VINTNERS' PLACE, EC4

In an area which by the tenth century already had such a large population of French wine sellers that it became known as the Vintry, this is also the site of the Hall of the Worshipful Company of Vintners. As long ago as 1364 its members enjoyed a monopoly on trade with Gascony in wine, cloth and herrings – but they have since specialised and ditched the fish.

WATERGATE, EC4

Now an unlovely, shapeless cul-de-sac built on the site of the water-gate to the palace of Bridewell.

WHITTINGTON AVENUE, EC3

A route into Leadenhall Market, the rights to which belonged to Sir Richard Whittington in 1411.

WORMWOOD STREET, EC2

As with Camomile Court, the name refers to the plant *Artemisia absinthium*, which grew here and was favoured for its presumed ability to remedy indigestion and alleviate gastric and labour pains.

Appendix II

THE CITY OF LONDON WARDS

With the Corporation of London, the municipal governing body of the City of London, the area we know as the Square Mile is divided into twenty-five electoral wards. As their often colourful names indicate, the wards are ancient subdivisions, many dating back to Norman times, so that over the last 1,000 years or so their number has scarcely changed. In 1206 there were twenty-four of them, and today the total has been increased by just one by the division (as recently as 1394) of Farrington into Farringdon Within and Farringdon Without. Apparently this was done because 'the governance thereof is too laborious and grievous for one person to occupy and duly govern the same'.

Each ward is represented by a number of members determined by the size of the electorate, the total for each ward being made up by an Alderman and between two and ten Common Councilmen. Meetings known as wardmotes are held on the first Friday of September, on which occasion 'good and discreet citizens' are elected to the City's Court of Common Council.

1   Aldersgate
2   Aldgate
3   Bassishaw
4   Billingsgate
5   Bishopsgate
6   Bread Street
7   Bridge
8   Broad Street
9   Candlewick
10 Castle Baynard
11 Cheap
12 Coleman Street
13 Cordwainer
14 Cornhill
15 Cripplegate
16 Dowgate
17 Farringdon Within
18 Farringdon Without
19 Langbourn
20 Lime Street
21 Portsoken
22 Queenhithe
23 Tower
24 Vintry
25 Walbrook

CITY OF LONDON PARISHES

Because each parish within the historic City of London comprises at most only a street or two, they are sensibly named after the relevant churches rather than their geographical location. Some confusion still arises, however, because several dedications are used more than once – All Hallows, St Andrew, even St Botolph – and because a great number of churches no longer survive.

All Hallows Barking-by-the-Tower
All Hallows Bread Street
All Hallows Honey Lane
All Hallows Lombard Street
All Hallows on the Wall
All Hallows Staining
All Hallows the Great
All Hallows the Less
All Saints Skinner Street
Bridewell Chapel
Christchurch Newgate Street
Holy Trinity Gough Square
Holy Trinity Minories

Holy-Trinity-the-Less
St Alban Wood Street
St Alphage London Wall
St Andrew-by-the-Wardrobe
St Andrew Holborn
St Andrew Hubbard
St Andrew Undershaft
St Ann Blackfriars
St Anne and St Agnes
St Antholin Budge Row
St Augustine Watling Street
St Bartholomew-by-the-Exchange
St Bartholomew Moor Lane

St Bartholomew-the-Great
St Bartholomew-the-Less
St Benet Fink
St Benet Gracechurch
St Benet Paul's Wharf
St Benet Sherehog
St Botolph Without
 Aldersgate
St Botolph Without Aldgate
St Botolph Billingsgate
St Botolph-Without-
 Bishopsgate
St Bride Fleet Street
St Christopher le Stocks
St Clement Eastcheap
St Dionis Backchurch
St Dunstan-in-the-East
St Dunstan-in-the-West
St Edmund the King
 and Martyr
St Ethelburga Bishopsgate
St Ewin
St Faith under St Paul
St Gabriel Fenchurch Street
St George Botolph Lane
St Giles Cripplegate
St Gregory by St Paul
St Helen Bishopsgate
St James Duke's Place
St James Garlickhythe
St John the Baptist Walbrook

St John the Evangelist
 Friday Street
St John Zachary
St Katherine Coleman
St Katherine Cree
St Laurence Pountney
St Lawrence Jewry-
 next-Guildhall
St Leonard Eastcheap
St Leonard Foster Lane
St Magnus the Martyr
St Margaret Lothbury
St Margaret Moses
St Margaret New Fish Street
St Margaret Pattens
St Martin Ludgate
St Martin Orgar
St Martin Outwich
St Martin Pomeroy
St Martin Vintry
St Mary Abchurch
St Mary Aldermanbury
St Mary Aldermary
St Mary-At-Hill
St Mary Axe
St Mary Bothaw
St Mary Colechurch
St Mary-le-Bow
St Mary Magdalen Milk Street
St Mary Magdalen Old
 Fish Street

St Mary Mounthaw
St Mary Somerset
St Mary Staining
St Mary Woolchurch Haw
St Mary Woolnoth
St Matthew Friday Street
St Michael Bassishaw
St Michael Cornhill
St Michael Crooked Lane
St Michael le Querne
St Michael Paternoster Royal
St Michael Queenhithe
St Michael Wood Street
St Mildred Bread Street
St Mildred Poultry
St Nicholas Acons
St Nicholas Cole Abbey
St Nicholas Olave
St Nicholas Shambles

St Olave Hart Street
St Olave Upwell Old Jewry
St Olave Silver Street
St Pancras Soper Lane
St Peter Cornhill
St Peter-le-Poer
St Peter Paul's Wharf
St Peter Westcheap
St Sepulchre-Without-
   Newgate
St Stephen Coleman Street
St Stephen Walbrook
St Swithin London Stone
St Thomas Apostle
St Thomas in the Liberty of
   the Rolls
St Vedast Foster Lane
Temple Church

Appendix IV

BUILT, BURNED, REBUILT, BOMBED AND REDUNDANT

THE FATE OF CITY CHURCHES

In today's dramatically depopulated City the number of churches seems high. Before the Great Fire there were many more, however, with something like 100 towers and spires dominating the skyline of the walled city. Of these, ninety-seven were parish churches, eighty-nine of which fell to the flames. An Act of Parliament passed in 1670 required that fifty-one of those that had been destroyed be rebuilt in the following years.

Since then further losses have been incurred, and not only during the Second World War, and at the same time parishes and congregations have continued to merge as the population has dwindled. Today a mere thirty-eight churches survive, although with a residential population of around 8,000 – barely 4 per cent of its eighteenth-century peak, and the vast majority living in the Barbican – the number of regular worshippers within the Square Mile must be at an all-time low.

ALL HALLOWS BARKING-BY-THE-TOWER
Great Tower Street
Saxon. Damaged 1666, rebuilt, destroyed 1940. Rebuilt again 1957.

ALL HALLOWS BREAD STREET
Thirteenth century, destroyed 1666, rebuilt by Wren, demolished 1876.

ALL HALLOWS HONEY LANE
Thirteenth century, destroyed 1666 and not rebuilt.

ALL HALLOWS LOMBARD STREET
Eleventh century, destroyed 1666, rebuilt by Wren, sold 1938.

ALL HALLOWS ON THE WALL
Twelfth century, built on the foundations of the Roman wall, the circular vestry describing the semi-circular shape of the bastion beneath. Destroyed 1666, rebuilt 1765–67 by George Dance the Younger (very much the younger, he was 24 at the time).

ALL HALLOWS STAINING
Mark Lane
Twelfth century, collapsed in 1671 having survived the Great Fire. Rebuilt but demolished in 1870 leaving only the crypt and tower.

ALL HALLOWS THE GREAT
Upper Thames Street
Thirteenth century, destroyed 1666, rebuilt by Wren, demolished 1894 except for tower. Also known as All Hallows in La Corderie and All Hallows at the Hay.

ALL HALLOWS THE LESS
Upper Thames Street
Thirteenth century, destroyed 1666 and not rebuilt. Also known as All Hallows-Upon-the Cellar.

ALL SAINTS SKINNER STREET
1864. United with St Botolph Bishopsgate five years later.

BRIDEWELL CHAPEL
United with St Bride Fleet Street 1864

CHRISTCHURCH NEWGATE STREET
1547. Destroyed 1666, rebuilt by Wren 1677–91 using some medieval materials, gutted in 1940. Tower restored in 1960 and more recently converted to private dwelling.

HOLY TRINITY GOUGH SQUARE
Built 1842 by J. Shaw. Merged with St Bride Fleet Street in 1906.

HOLY TRINITY MINORIES
Destroyed 1666, rebuilt 1706, bombed 1940 and sold. Merged with St Botolph Aldgate.

HOLY-TRINITY-THE-LESS
Knightrider Street
Destroyed 1666 and not rebuilt. Merged with St Michael Queenhithe in 1670.

LAMBE'S CHAPEL
Monkwell Street

Also known as St James-in-the-Wall. Demolished in 1872 and the crypt removed to Star Alley.

OLD RED HAND AND MITRE CHAPEL (NON-PAROCHIAL)

An informal chapel in the vicinity of Fleet prison where clandestine marriages were performed until 1754.

ROYAL CHAPEL OF ST JOHN

Within the White Tower. Built *c.* 1080.

ST ALBAN WOOD STREET

Destroyed 1666, rebuilt by Wren 1682–87, destroyed 1940. Tower remains as private dwelling.

ST ALPHAGE LONDON WALL

Damaged 1666, rebuilt 1777, demolished 1924. Tower remains on Roman base. Merged with St Giles Cripplegate in 1954.

ST ANDREW-BY-THE-WARDROBE
Queen Victoria Street

Destroyed 1666, rebuilt by Wren 1685–95, damaged 1940.

ST ANDREW HOLBORN

Destroyed 1666, rebuilt by Wren 1687, damaged 1941, rebuilt 1960.

ST ANDREW HUBARD
Philpot Lane

Destroyed 1666 and not rebuilt. Merged with St Mary-at-Hill 1670.

ST ANDREW UNDERSHAFT
Leadenhall Street

Bombed 1992.

ST ANN BLACKFRIARS

Destroyed 1666 and not rebuilt. Merged with St Andrew-by-the-Wardrobe in 1670.

ST ANNE AND ST AGNES
Gresham Street

Destroyed 1666, rebuilt by Wren 1676–87, damaged in the Second World War, rebuilt 1966. Merged with St Vedast Foster Lane in 1954.

ST ANTHOLIN BUDGE ROW

Destroyed 1666, rebuilt by Wren, sold 1874, demolished 1875. Merged with St Mary Aldermary in 1873.

ST AUGUSTINE WATLING STREET

Destroyed 1666, rebuilt by Wren 1680–87. Bombed 1941, tower only remains. Merged with St Mary-le-Bow in 1954.

ST BARTHOLOMEW-BY-THE-EXCHANGE

Destroyed 1666, rebuilt by Wren, demolished 1902. Merged with St Margaret Lothbury in 1839.

ST BARTHOLOMEW MOORE LANE

1850. Merged with St Giles Cripplegate in 1900.

ST BARTHOLOMEW-THE-GREAT
Little Britain

Established as part of a priory in 1123. Restored by Sir Aston Webb, nineteenth century.

ST BARTHOLOMEW-THE-LESS
Little Britain

1184. Bombed in Second World War but repaired and reopened in 1951.

ST BENET FINK
Threadneedle Street

Destroyed 1666, rebuilt by Wren, demolished 1844. Merged with St Peter le Poer in 1842, then St Michael Cornhill in 1906.

ST BENET GRACECHURCH

Destroyed 1666, rebuilt by Wren, demolished 1867. Merged with All Hallows Lombard Street in 1864, and St Edmund the King and Martyr in 1937.

ST BENET PAUL'S WHARF
Queen Victoria Street

Destroyed 1666, rebuilt by Wren 1677–85. Merged with St Nicholas Cole Abbey in 1879.

ST BENET SHEREHOG
Poultry
Destroyed 1666 and not rebuilt. Merged with St Stephen Walbrook 1670.

ST BOTOLPH ALDERSGATE
Aldersgate Street
Also known as St Botolph Without Aldersgate. Destroyed 1666, rebuilt 1788 by Nathaniel Wright.

ST BOTOLPH ALDGATE
Aldgate High Street
Also known as St Botolph Without Aldgate. Destroyed 1666, rebuilt 1741 by George Dance the Elder.

ST BOTOLPH BILLINGSGATE
Destroyed 1666 and not rebuilt. Merged with St George Botolph Lane in 1670, St Mary-at-Hill in 1901.

ST BOTOLPH BISHOPSGATE
Damaged 1666, rebuilt 1725 by James Gold.

ST BRIDE FLEET STREET
Destroyed 1666, rebuilt by Wren 1670–84, gutted in the Second World War and rebuilt.

ST CHRISTOPHER LE STOCKS
Threadneedle Street
Destroyed 1666, rebuilt by Wren, demolished 1781. Merged with St Margaret Lothbury in 1781.

ST CLEMENT EASTCHEAP
King William Street
Destroyed 1666, rebuilt by Wren 1683–87.

ST DIONIS BACKCHURCH
Langbourn Ward
Destroyed 1666, rebuilt by Wren, demolished 1878. Merged with All Hallows Lombard Street in 1876, and St Edmund the King and Martyr in 1937.

ST DUNSTAN-IN-THE-EAST
St Dunstan's Alley
Rebuilt 1817–21, gutted in 1941. Tower only remaining, converted to clinic. Remainder of ruin now a garden. Merged with All Hallows Barking-by-the-Tower in 1960.

ST DUNSTAN-IN-THE-WEST
Fleet Street
Eleventh century. Rebuilt by John Shaw and John Shaw Jr 1831–33.

ST EDMUND THE KING AND MARTYR
Lombard Street
Built by Wren 1670–79.

ST ETHELBURGA BISHOPSGATE
1250 and rebuilt in 1390. Bombed 1993 and rebuilt 1993–2002.

ST EWIN
Warwick Lane
Also known as St Audoen-within-Newgate. Demolished at the Dissolution.

ST FAITH UNDER ST PAUL

Destroyed 1666 and not rebuilt. Merged with St Augustine Watling Street 1670, and St Mary-le-Bow 1954.

ST GABRIEL FENCHURCH

Destroyed 1666 and not rebuilt. Merged with St Margaret Pattens in 1670.

ST GEORGE BOTOLPH LANE

Destroyed 1666, rebuilt by Wren, demolished 1901.

ST GILES CRIPPLEGATE

Fore Street

Damaged in the Second World War, rebuilt 1953–63.

ST GREGORY BY ST PAUL

Rebuilt 1641–50, destroyed 1666, merged with St Mary Magdalen Old Fish Street in 1670, and St Martin Ludgate in 1890.

ST HELEN BISHOPSGATE

1290. Damaged by terrorist bomb in 1992.

ST JAMES DUKE'S PLACE

1622, demolished 1874, merged with St Katherine Cree, 1873.

ST JAMES GARLICKHYTHE

Upper Thames Street

Wren 1676–82. The church registers, dating back to 1535, are almost certainly London's oldest.

ST JOHN THE BAPTIST WALBROOK

Destroyed 1666 and not rebuilt. Merged with St Antholin Budge Row in 1670, and St Mary Aldermary in 1873.

ST JOHN THE EVANGELIST FRIDAY STREET

Destroyed 1666 and not rebuilt. Merged with All Hallows Bread Street in 1670, St Mary-le-Bow in 1876.

ST JOHN ZACHARY

Gresham Street

Destroyed 1666 and not rebuilt. Merged with St Anne and St Agnes in 1670, and St Vedast Foster Lane in 1954.

ST KATHERINE COLEMAN

Destroyed 1666, rebuilt 1738–41, demolished 1926. Merged with St Olave Hart Street in 1921.

ST KATHERINE CREE

Leadenhall Street

1108, rebuilt 1631, restored 1962.

ST LAURENCE POUNTNEY

Destroyed 1666 and not rebuilt. Merged with St Mary Abchurch in 1670.

ST LAWRENCE JEWRY-NEXT-GUILDHALL

Gresham Street

Wren 1670–87.

ST LEONARD EASTCHEAP

Destroyed 1666 and not rebuilt. Merged with St Benet Gracechurch in 1670, All Hallows Lombard Street in 1864, St Edmund the King and Martyr in 1937.

ST LEONARD FOSTER LANE

Destroyed 1666 and not rebuilt. Merged with Christchurch Newgate Street 1670, St Sepulchre-without-Newgate 1954.

ST MAGNUS THE MARTYR
Lower Thames Street

Early twelfth century, destroyed in 1666, rebuilt by Wren 1671–87.

ST MARGARET LOTHBURY

Twelfth century, destroyed in 1666, rebuilt by Wren 1686–1700.

ST MARGARET MOSES
Little Friday Street

Destroyed 1666 and not rebuilt. Merged with St Mildred Bread Street in 1670, St Mary-le-Bow in 1954.

ST MARGARET NEW FISH STREET

Destroyed 1666 and not rebuilt. Merged with St Magnus the Martyr in 1670.

ST MARGARET PATTENS
Eastcheap

1067, rebuilt in stone, demolished in 1530. It was rebuilt in 1538, destroyed in 1666 and rebuilt by Wren in 1684.

ST MARTIN LUDGATE

Struck by lightning in 1571, destroyed in 1666, rebuilt by Wren 1677–87.

ST MARTIN ORGAR

Cannon Street

Damaged 1666 and demolished in 1820. Tower only rebuilt 1851.

ST MARTIN OUTWICH

Threadneedle Street

Destroyed 1666, rebuilt 1796, sold 1874. Merged with St Helen Bishopsgate in 1873.

ST MARTIN POMEROY

Ironmonger Lane

Destroyed 1666 and not rebuilt. Merged with St Olave Upwell Old Jewry in 1670, St Margaret Lothbury in 1886.

ST MARTIN VINTRY

Upper Thames Street

Destroyed 1666 and not rebuilt. Merged with St Michael Paternoster Royal in 1670.

ST MARY ABCHURCH

Cannon Street

Twelfth century, rebuilt by Wren 1681–87.

ST MARY ALDERMANBURY

Destroyed 1666, rebuilt by Wren, destroyed 1940, remains sent to USA. Merged with St Alphage London Wall in 1917, St Giles Cripplegate in 1954.

ST MARY ALDERMARY
Queen Victoria Street
1510, destroyed in 1666, rebuilt by Wren 1682, tower 1701.

ST MARY-AT-HILL
Lovat Lane
Fourteenth century, destroyed 1666, rebuilt by Wren 1670–76, tower 1780, interior 1843. Reached via a narrow doorway at the peculiar Victorian Peek House.

ST MARY AXE
Leadenhall Street
Demolished 1561. Merged with St Andrew Undershaft.

ST MARY BOTHAW
Cannon Street
Destroyed 1666 and not rebuilt. Merged with St Swithin London Stone in 1670, and St Stephen Walbrook in 1954.

ST MARY COLECHURCH
Destroyed 1666 and not rebuilt. Merged with St Mildred Poultry in 1670, St Olave Upwell Old Jewry in 1871 and St Margaret Lothbury in 1886.

ST MARY-LE-BOW
Cheapside
Norman, destroyed in 1666, rebuilt by Wren 1670–83, gutted 1941 and rebuilt.

ST MARY MAGDALEN MILK STREET

Thirteenth century, destroyed 1666 and not rebuilt. Merged with St Lawrence Jewry-next-Guildhall in 1670.

ST MARY MAGDALEN OLD FISH STREET

Twelfth century, destroyed 1666, rebuilt by Wren, damaged by fire 1886, demolished 1887. Merged with St Martin Ludgate in 1890.

ST MARY MOUNTHAW
Old Fish Street Hill

Destroyed 1666 and not rebuilt. Merged with St Mary Somerset in 1670, and St Nicholas Cole Abbey in 1866.

ST MARY SOMERSET
Upper Thames Street

Damaged 1666, rebuilt by Wren 1695, demolished in 1872 with tower remaining and at time of writing is being converted to a private dwelling. Merged with St Nicholas Cole Abbey in 1866.

ST MARY STAINING
Oat Lane

Twelfth century. Destroyed 1666 and not rebuilt. Merged with St Michael Wood Street in 1670, St Alban Wood Street in 1894, and St Vedast Foster Lane in 1954.

ST MARY WOOLCHURCH HAW
On the site of Mansion House

Destroyed 1666 and not rebuilt. Merged with St Mary Woolnoth 1670.

ST MARY WOOLNOTH
Lombard Street

Twelfth century, destroyed in 1666, rebuilt by Hawksmoor 1716–26.

ST MATTHEW FRIDAY STREET

Thirteenth century, destroyed 1666, rebuilt by Wren, sold 1881, demolished 1885. Merged with St Vedast Foster Lane 1882.

ST MICHAEL BASSISHAW
Basinghall Street

Twelfth century, destroyed 1666, rebuilt by Wren, sold 1899, demolished 1900. Merged with St Lawrence Jewry-next-Guildhall in 1897.

ST MICHAEL CORNHILL

Eleventh century, destroyed 1666, rebuilt by Wren begun 1672, tower added by Hawksmoor 1718–24.

ST MICHAEL CROOKED LANE

Thirteenth century, destroyed 1666 rebuilt by Wren, sold 1831, demolished. Merged with St Magnus the Martyr in 1831.

ST MICHAEL LE QUERNE

Twelfth century, destroyed 1666 and not rebuilt. Also known as St Michael at Corn. Merged with St Vedast Foster Lane.

ST MICHAEL PATERNOSTER ROYAL
College Hill

Thirteenth century, destroyed 1666, rebuilt by Wren 1686–94.

ST MICHAEL QUEENHITHE
Upper Thames Street

Twelfth century, destroyed 1666, rebuilt by Wren, demolished 1875. Merged with St James Garlickhythe in 1875.

ST MICHAEL WOOD STREET

Thirteenth century, destroyed 1666, rebuilt by Wren, demolished 1897. Merged with St Alban Wood Street in 1894, and St Vedast Foster Lane in 1954.

ST MILDRED BREAD STREET

Thirteenth century, destroyed 1666, rebuilt by Wren, destroyed 1940 and not rebuilt despite being the only Wren interior to have escaped so-called improvement. The site was sold and the congregation merged with St Mary-le-Bow in 1954.

ST MILDRED POULTRY

Twelfth century, destroyed 1666, rebuilt by Wren, sold 1872 and demolished. Merged with St Olave Upwell Old Jewry in 1871, and St Margaret Lothbury in 1886.

ST NICHOLAS ACONS
By Lombard Street and Cannon Street

Eleventh century, destroyed 1666 and not rebuilt. Merged with St Edmund the King and Martyr in 1670.

ST NICHOLAS BY THE SHAMBLES
Newgate Street

Amalgamated with St Ewin to form Christchurch Newgate Street in 1547.

ST NICHOLAS COLE ABBEY
Queen Victoria Street

The first church to be rebuilt by Wren (1671), costing £5,042 including £2 14*s* for the architect's dinner and a sixpence for half a pint of canary sack for his coachmen.

ST NICHOLAS OLAVE
Broad Street Hill

Eleventh century, destroyed 1666 and not rebuilt. Merged with St Nicholas Cole Abbey in 1670.

ST OLAVE HART STREET
Fenchurch Street

Fifteenth century, survived 1666 but seriously damaged in 1941. Restoration completed in 1951.

ST OLAVE UPWELL OLD JEWRY
Poultry

Destroyed 1666, rebuilt by Wren 1670–76, demolished in 1888–1891 but for tower. Merged with St Margaret Lothbury in 1886.

ST OLAVE SILVER STREET
Noble Street

Destroyed 1666 and not rebuilt. Merged with St Alban Wood Street in 1670, and St Vedast Foster Lane in 1954.

ST PANCRAS SOPER LANE

Thirteenth century, destroyed 1666 and not rebuilt. Merged with St Mary-le-Bow in 1670.

ST PETER AD VINCULA

Within the precincts of the Tower of London. Built in twelfth century, rebuilt in the sixteenth.

ST PETER CORNHILL

Date unknown but rebuilt by Wren 1667–87, restored by J.D. Wyatt 1872.

ST PETER-LE-POER
Old Broad Street

Twelfth century, rebuilt 1792, sold 1907 and demolished. Merged with St Michael Cornhill in 1906.

ST PETER PAUL'S WHARF
Upper Thames Street

Twelfth century, destroyed 1666 and not rebuilt. Merged with St Benet Paul's Wharf in 1670, and St Nicholas Cole Abbey in 1879.

ST PETER WESTCHEAP
Wood Street

Fifteenth century, destroyed 1666 and not rebuilt, part of churchyard remains. Merged with St Matthew Friday Street in 1670, St Vedast Foster Lane in 1882.

ST SEPULCHRE-WITHOUT-NEWGATE
Holborn Viaduct

Twelfth century, gutted in 1666, restored 1878. The largest parish church in the City, it houses the bell which tolled the night before executions at Newgate Prison.

ST STEPHEN COLEMAN
Coleman Street

Thirteenth century, perhaps for a time a synagogue. Destroyed 1666, rebuilt by Wren, damaged in 1940 and the site sold. Merged with St Margaret Lothbury in 1954.

ST STEPHEN WALBROOK

Eleventh century, destroyed in 1666, rebuilt by Wren 1672–77.

ST SWITHIN LONDON STONE
Cannon Street

Fifteenth century, destroyed 1666, rebuilt by Wren, and destroyed again in 1940. Merged with St Stephen Walbrook in 1954.

ST THOMAS IN THE LIBERTY OF THE ROLLS

Rebuilt 1842, sold 1882. Merged with St Dunstan-in-the-West in 1886.

ST THOMAS THE APOSTLE
Queen Street

Twelfth century, destroyed 1666 and not rebuilt. Merged with St Mary Aldermary 1670.

ST VEDAST-ALIAS-FOSTER
Foster Lane

Twelfth century, destroyed 1666, rebuilt by Wren 1695–1700, damaged in 1941, restored 1962.

TEMPLE CHURCH

Twelfth century, undamaged in the Great Fire but refurbished by Wren. Damaged in 1941, rededicated in 1958.

CITY OPEN SPACES

Besides owning more than 10,000 acres of wood- and heathland, including the great expanses of Epping Forest, Burnham Beeches and Hampstead Heath, the City of London by its own estimates manages more than 200 individual parks, gardens, churchyards and squares within the Square Mile. Many are mentioned in the main text, some are barely more than the proverbial pocket-handkerchief, but in one of the most built-up areas of the capital even the tiniest patch of green is to be welcomed by city workers, visitors and wildlife.

Abchurch Yard, Abchurch Lane
Aldermanbury Square
Aldermanbury/Gresham
    Street
Aldermanbury/Love Lane
All Hallows Barking-by-the-
    Tower
All Hallows London Wall
Barbers' Hall Herb Garden
Bastion House/Roman Wall
Bishopsgate Churchyard
Blackfriars Bridge, South
    Garden
Bow Churchyard

Brewers' Hall
Bridgewater Square
Bunhill Fields
Carter Lane Information
    Centre
Christchurch Greyfriars
    Church Garden
Christchurch Greyfriars
    Churchyard
Church Entry
Devonshire Square
Dutch Church, Austin Friars
Fann Street Wildlife Garden,
    Beech Street

Fen Court, Fenchurch Street
Fenchurch Place
Fenn Court (St Gabriel's Fen)
Festival Gardens, St Paul's
    Cathedral
Finsbury Circus Gardens
Ireland Yard
Jubilee Garden, Houndsditch
Newgate Street Garden
Noble Street Gardens
Old Change Court
Peters Hill St Paul's Vista
Portsoken Street Garden
Princess Alice Garden, St
    Bartholomew-the-Less
Seething Lane Garden
Smithfield Rotunda Garden
St Alphage's Garden London
    Wall
St Andrew Holborn
St Andrew-by-the-Wardrobe
St Andrew's Churchyard,
    Holborn
St Andrew's Undershaft
St Anne and St Agnes
St Bartholomew-the-Great
St Benet Fink
St Benet Paul's Wharf
St Benet's Church Garden
St Botolph Aldgate
St Bride Fleet Street

St Clement Eastcheap
St Dunstan-in-the-East
St Dunstan-in-the-West
St Giles' Terrace
St Helen Bishopsgate
St James Garlickhythe
St Katharine Cree
St Magnus the Martyr
St Mary Aldermanbury
St Mary Aldermary
St Mary-at-Hill
St Mary-le-Bow Church
    Garden
St Mary Somerset
St Mary Staining
St Mary Woolnoth
St Michael Cornhill
St Michael Paternoster
    Royal
St Olave Upwell Old Jewry
St Olave Noble Street
St Olave Hart Street
St Paul's Choir School
St Paul's Churchyard
St Paul's Cathedral
St Peter Cheap
St Peter's Westcheap
St Peter's Cornhill
St Sepulchre-without-
    Newgate
St Swithin's Oxford Court

St Vedast Alias Foster
Swan Lane Riverside Walk
Tower Hill Garden

West Smithfield
Whittington Gardens, Upper
    Thames Street

BIBLIOGRAPHY

Unless otherwise stated all books are published in London.

Allinson, Ken, *London's Contemporary Architecture*, Architectural Press, 2006

Arnold, Catherine, *Necropolis: London and its Dead*, Simon & Schuster, 2006

Arnold-Baker, Charles, *The Companion to British History*, Longcross Press, Tunbridge Wells, 1996

Barker, F. & Silvester-Carr, D., *The Black Plaque Guide to London*, Constable & Co., 1987

Barker, F. & Jackson, P., *London: 2000 Years of a City and its People*, Cassell, 1974

Brook, Stephen, *The Club: The Jews of Modern Britain*, Constable, 1989

Bryant, Sir Arthur, *Samuel Pepys: The Saviour of the Navy*, William Collins, 1953

Burke, John, *Look Back on England*, Orbis, 1980

Burton, N. & Guillery, P., *Behind the Façade London House Plans 1660–1840*, Spire, Reading, 2006

Cannadine, David, *The Decline and Fall of the British Aristocracy*, Yale, New Haven, 1990

Clark, Sir G. (ed.), *The Oxford History of England* (16 vols), Oxford University Press, Oxford, 1975

Clout, Hugh (ed.), *The Times London History Atlas*, Times Books, 1991

Clunn, Harold P., *The Face of London*, Spring Books, 1957

Cocroft, W. & Thomas, J., *Cold War: Building for Nuclear Confrontation 1946–1989*, English Heritage, Swindon, 2004

Cunnington, Pamela, *Change of Use*, A&C Black, 1988

Dictionary of National Biography, Oxford University Press, Oxford, 1975

Duncan, Andrew, *Secret London*, New Holland, 2003

Durant, G.M., *Britain: Rome's Most Northerly Province*, G. Bell & Sons, 1969

Earl, Peter, *A City Full of People: The Men and Women of London 1650–1750*, Methuen, 1994

Fairfield, Sheila, *The Streets of London: A Dictionary of the Names and Their Origins*, Papermac, 1983

Fellows, Richard, *Edwardian Architecture: Style and Technology*, Lund Humphries, 1995

Fletcher, Sir Banister, *A History of Architecture on the Comparative Method*, 18th edition, Athlone Press, 1975

Fletcher, Geoffrey, *The London Nobody Knows*, Penguin, 1965
—— *London At My Feet*, Daily Telegraph, 1980

Foxell, Simon, *Mapping London: Making Sense of the City*, Black Dog, 2007

Frere, Sheppard, *Britannia: A History of Roman Britain*, Routledge & Kegan Paul, 1967

Friar, Stephen, *The Companion to English Parish Churches*, Sutton, Stroud, 1996

Galinou, Mireille (ed.), *London's Pride: The Glorious History of the Capital's Garden*, Anaya, 1990

Greenwood, Douglas, *Who's Buried Where in England*, Constable, 1982

Halliday, Stephen, *Newgate: London's Prototype of Hell*, Sutton, Stroud, 2006

Hanson, Neil, *The Dreadful Judgement: The True Story of the Great Fire of London*, Doubleday, 2001

Hibbert, Christopher, *London: The Biography of a City*, Longmans, 1969
—— *The Personal History of Samuel Johnson*, Longmans, 1971
—— , Weinreb, B. & Keay, J., *The London Encyclopaedia*, 3rd edition, Macmillan, 2008

Hobhouse, Hermione, *Lost London*, Weathervane Books, New York, 1971

Hope, Valerie, *My Lord Mayor: Eight Hundred Years of London's Mayorality*, Weidenfeld & Nicolson, 1989
—— , Birch, C. & Torry, G., *The Freedom: The Past and Present of the Livery, Guilds and City of London*, Barracuda Books, Buckingham, 1982

Howard, Phillip, *We Thundered Out: 200 Years of The Times*, Times Books, 1985

Hudson, Roger, *London: Portrait of a City*, Folio Society, 1998

Inwood, Stephen, *Historic London: An Explorer's Companion*, Macmillan, 2008

Jackson, Peter, *Walks in Old London*, Brockhampton Press, 1995

Jardine, Lisa, *Ingenious Pursuits: Building the Scientific Revolution*, Little, Brown, 1999

Jenkins, Simon, *City at Risk: A Contemporary Look at London's Streets*, Hutchinson, 1970

—— *England's Thousand Best Churches*, Allen Lane, 1999

Jenner, Michael, *The Architectural Heritage of Britain & Ireland*, Michael Joseph, 1995

—— *London Heritage: The Changing Style of a City*, Michael Joseph, 1988

Johnson, Nichola, *Eighteenth Century London*, HMSO, 1991

Jones, E. & Woodward, C., *A Guide to the Architecture of London*, Seven Dials, 2000

Kent, William, *An Encyclopaedia of London*, Dent, 1970

Kerr, Nigel (ed.), *John Betjeman's Guide to English Parish Churches*, HarperCollins, 1993

—— & Kerr, M., *A Guide to Medieval Sites in Britain*, Diamond Books, 1988

Kightly, Charles, *The Customs and Ceremonies of Britain*, Thames & Hudson, 1986

Leapman, Michael (ed.), *The Book of London*, Weidenfeld & Nicolson, 1992

Long, David, *London's 100 Most Extraordinary Buildings*, The History Press, Stroud, 2018

—— *London's 100 Strangest Places*, The History Press, Stroud, 2018

—— *The Little Book of London*, The History Press, Stroud, 2007

Marsden, Peter, *The Roman Forum Site in London: Discoveries before 1985*, HMSO, 1987

Mee, Arthur, *London: Heart of the Empire and Wonder of the World*, Hodder & Stoughton, 1937

Merullo, Annabel (ed.), *British Greats*, Cassell, 2000

Milne, Gustav, *Book of Roman London: Urban Archaeology in the Nation's Capital*, English Heritage/B.T. Batsford, 1995

Moore, Tim, *Do Not Pass Go: From the Old Kent Road to Mayfair*, Vintage, 2003

Mordaunt Crook, J., *The Greek Revival: Neo-Classical Attitudes in British Architecture 1760–1870*, RIBA/Country Life, 1968

Mount, Harry, *A Lust for Window Sills: A Lover's Guide to British Buildings from Portcullis to Pebble-Dash*, Little, Brown, 2008

Nicolson, Nigel (ed.), *The Harold Nicolson Diaries and Letters 1907–1964*, Weidenfeld & Nicolson, 2004

Pearce, David, *The Great Houses of London*, The Vendome Press, 1986

Pevsner, Nikolaus, *Buildings of England: The Cities of London and Westminster*, Penguin, 1957

Picard, Liza, *Dr Johnson's London: Life in London, 1740–1770*, Weidenfeld & Nicolson, 2000

—— *Elizabeth's London: Everyday Life in Elizabethan London*, Weidenfeld & Nicolson, 2003

—— *Restoration London*, Weidenfeld & Nicolson, 1997

—— *Victorian London: The Life of a City 1840–1870*, Weidenfeld & Nicolson, 2005

Plimmer, C. & Plimmer, D., *London: A Visitor's Companion*, Batsford, 1977

Pollins, Harold, *Economic History of the Jews in England*, Associated University Presses, 1982

Pottle, F.A. (ed.), *Boswell's London Journal 1762–1763*, Heinemann, 1950

Powell, Kenneth, *New London Architecture*, Merrell, 2001

—— *New London Architecture 2*, Merrell, 2007

Rowlandson, T. & Pugin, A.C., *The Microcosm of London*, King Penguin, 1947

Saint, A. & Darley, G., *The Chronicles of London*, Weidenfeld & Nicolson, 1994

Saunders, Ann, *The Art and Architecture of London: An Illustrated Guide*, Phaidon, Oxford, 1988

—— *St Paul's: The Story of a Cathedral*, Collins & Brown, 2001

Simon, Kate, *London Places and Pleasures: An Uncommon Guidebook*, MacGibbon & Kee, 1968

Stamp, Gavin, *The Changing Metropolis: Earliest Photographs of London 1839–79*, Viking, 1984

Stow, John, *A Survey of London*, 1598

Strong, Roy, *Lost Treasures of Britain*, Viking, 1990

—— *The Renaissance Garden in England*, Thames & Hudson, 1979

Summerson, John, *Georgian London*, Yale University Press, New Haven, 2003

Sutton, Anne, *The Mercery of London: Trade, Goods and People, 1130–1578*, Ashgate, Aldershot, 2005

Thompson, J. & Sturrock, J., *New Heart for an Old Soul: Spitalfields Revitalised*, Spitalfields Development Group, 2009

Thorold, Peter, *The London Rich: The Creation of a Great City from 1666 to the Present*, Viking, 1999